'This book does what it says on the ti...  ...ly explores the deepest iss... good look around the l... the questions we all hav... response, but instead en... and gently leads us throu... ...on. Using personal experience, ane... ...a wide variety of sources and perspectives, Patrick brings us not to a set of answers, or a quick formula for a shallow solution. He simply presents God's heart of love; God's goodness in the face of bad; God's strength in our weakness; God's healing for our hurts.'
Arianna Walker, Chief Executive, Mercy UK

'The power of this book is in its piercing honesty and vulnerability. It gives a voice to those issues that we as Christians sometimes want silenced: what happens when darkness falls? Where is God in mental illness? Can I ever be enough? Through Patrick's stories of his own life and those of others, he powerfully reminds us that a life of faith is smattered with, but not shattered by, dark places. This is an amazing book which will bless, encourage and comfort many.'
Tim and Rachel Hughes, Lead Pastors at Gas Street Church, Birmingham

'The Bible is way more honest than most churches about the actual levels of pain and confusion in life. That's why we need this book. It's going to provoke ten thousand honest conversations, helping to bring healing, hope and understanding to many who currently suffer in silence.'
Pete Greig, Founder of 24-7 Prayer and Leader of Emmaus Rd Church, Guildford

'When things are dark or difficult, it's good to know that you're not alone – others have been there and found that God was closer than ever. The stories and reflections in this hope-filled book point to a love that never lets us go.'
Paul Harcourt, National Leader of New Wine England and Author of *Walking on Water*

'Patrick Regan communicates heart to heart, which is one of the signs of the Holy Spirit. This is a humbling and deeply encouraging book.'
Lord Richard Chartres, Bishop of London

'"To be honest…" It's a phrase often on our lips, but often we're anything but honest about our struggles. In this raw, hopeful, visceral book, Patrick gently draws back the curtains, cracks opens the windows, and allows us all to breathe in the fresh air of vulnerability and reality. Don't miss it.'
Jeff Lucas, Author, Speaker and Broadcaster

'Patrick is the embodiment of authentic faith. This book will challenge, inspire, scare, and thrill you! Read it to discover deep and beautiful faith that embraces the truth that sets us all free.'
Danielle Strickland, Speaker, Author and Social Justice Advocate

'I have the privilege of knowing Patrick Regan not just as an inspirational leader, author and speaker, but as a friend. If I hadn't been his prayer partner, I am not sure I would have believed all the hardships he has faced, but they are all true. Equally true is his deep and totally uncynical faith in Jesus Christ and his hunger to engage in honest lament, and yet still love God and build His Church.'
Will van der Hart, Pastoral Chaplain at Holy Trinity Brompton (HTB)

'Honest, heartfelt and powerful. This important book is a must-read for anyone wanting to live a full and authentic life.'
Gavin Calver, Evangelical Alliance Director for Mission, England

'Patrick's book is full of unflinching lament at all that breaks and hurts us, and full of unswerving hope in a God who gathers all the broken pieces of our shattered bodies, minds, hopes and beliefs as He relentlessly loves and restores us. If you know what it's like to mourn, rage, wail, hope, despair and wait for God, then I recommend this book for your journey. It might just be one of the most significant books you read right now.'
Rachel Gardner, Director of National Work, Youthscape

'*Honesty Over Silence* contains vital truth for the Church today: we have to know (really know) that it's OK not to be OK. Patrick's honesty and vulnerability sets a wonderful example. None of us has it all together, and all of us have struggles. The book offers a timely encouragement that as a church community we should love one another through the hard times and learn to weep with those who weep. It is full of compassionate and practical advice on key areas like anxiety, depression and self-care, and ultimately reminds us that no matter what we are going through, we are not alone.'
Mike Pilavachi, Founder and Leader of Soul Survivor Church, Watford

'There can be a conspiracy of silence when it comes to brokenness. Leaders specifically, as well as Christians in general, can often feel ashamed or afraid to speak of their vulnerabilities, their fears, their disappointments or their shortcomings. To allow such a culture of silence to continue is to become complicit in maintaining a façade of faith, which is deadly and guilty of two great sins. The first is to perpetuate the myth that only the strong can be faithful, and the second is that to be honest is not as important as to be strong. These are deeply dangerous perspectives because they are not only wrong: they actually say the polar opposite to what Jesus and the Bible teach. It is only in being weak that we can allow God's strength to flow through us, and it is only in being honest that we can find a strength that is enduring – the strength of God rather than of human effort. *Honesty Over Silence* is a beautiful detonation of hope and grace that blows apart the prison walls of holding it all together and having to appear to be strong. And as the prison walls tumble around us, we are left with the shining light of God's comfort and nearness, bright and beautiful in the rays of grace and mercy.'
Rev Malcolm Duncan, Writer, Broadcaster, Pastor and Theologian in Residence at Spring Harvest

'Patrick Regan is an inspiration!'
Rob Parsons, OBE, Founder and Chairman of Care for the Family

'Physical pain, emotional anguish, loss, doubt, darkness – Patrick Regan has felt all this and more, sometimes all at once. Through it he has learnt that when you summon the bravery to vulnerably share your struggles, you end up giving others permission to be vulnerable too. And from that moment of connection, community gets formed, lessons are then shared, and we all start to heal. *Honesty Over Silence* will help you know what to let go of and what to hold on to as you walk your own wilderness journey.'
Sheridan Voysey, Writer, Speaker, Broadcaster and Author

'Patrick Regan has that rare ability of laying his weaknesses bare in a way that enables the sweet grace of Jesus to come through. As someone with a chronic illness, I found a kindred spirit who understood the depths of suffering but had dug deeper to find wisdom and hope. My copy of *Honesty Over Silence* is marked by tears and much underlining. It will move you; it will comfort you. Full of insight and gentle wisdom, this superb book is a perfect companion for anyone weakened by life, looking for God in it all, and needing to know they're not alone.'
Tanya Marlow, Writer, Broadcaster, Campaigner and Author

'We all eventually realise that life isn't like the fairytales we read as children – there are no guaranteed happy endings or gold-laden rainbows. Thankfully, in *Honesty Over Silence*, Patrick accompanies us past the easy answers, guiding us wisely along the tricky path of suffering that we all have to navigate at some point. You'll be better equipped for the journey with this helpful and honest book in your hands.'
Cathy Madavan, Writer, Speaker and Author

HONESTY

IT'S OK NOT TO BE OK

OVER

SILENCE

PATRICK REGAN

WITH **LIZA HOEKSMA**

CWR

Published 2018 by CWR, Waverley Abbey House, Waverley Lane, Farnham, Surrey
GU9 8EP, UK. CWR is a Registered Charity – Number 294387 and a Limited Company
registered in England – Registration Number 1990308.

For a list of National Distributors, visit www.cwr.org.uk/distributors

Scripture references are taken from the Holy Bible, New International Version®
Anglicised, NIV® Copyright ©1979, 1984, 2011 by Biblica, Inc.® Used by permission.
All rights reserved worldwide.

Scripture references marked NKJV taken from the New King James Version®.
Copyright © 1982 by Thomas Nelson. Used by permission. All rights reserved.

Concept development, editing, design and production by CWR.

Every effort has been made to ensure that this book contains the correct permissions
and references, but if anything has been inadvertently overlooked the Publisher will be
pleased to make the necessary arrangements at the first opportunity. Please contact the
Publisher directly.

Printed in the UK by Linney

ISBN: 978-1-78259-833-6

For Eddie and Mary Jane Donaldson,
whose love for each other and for God
continually inspired me. I hope this book
can be seen as just a tiny part of MJ's legacy:
the love, kindness and grace that she
gave to all of us.

I have a very special family, whose love, grace and dedication has been so amazing – Diane, Keziah, Daniel, Abigail, Caleb, Mum, Dad, Becky, John, David and Esther, Judy and Graham.

Special thanks to Liza – five books together! I love working with you, and the way you gently challenge me and make sure we come up with something hopefully very special.

To my special friends Johnny Sutherland, Will van der Hart and Andy Flanagan – your wisdom, advice and your joining me on the journey has been so valuable. Special thanks to Mike Coates, whose friendship and commitment to us for over 23 years is overwhelming. To all the team at XLP, especially Naomi Allen and my former EA, Lorna Dobbie for going the extra mile. Tara Cutland Green – I'm so grateful for all you've done. Thanks to the team at CWR, especially Mick and Lynette Brooks and Rebecca Berry – I'm so excited to be working with you. To the new team at Kintsugi Hope – Ludivine Kadimba, Sarah Davis, Louise Howitt, Pete and Nicki Sims, Adam and Hannah Temple, and special mention to our longest friends, Terry and Claudette Maragh.

A huge thank you to all my friends who so kindly endorsed this book, taking time out of their very busy schedules to read it – especially Christy Wimber, for doing the foreword.

CONTENTS

FOREWORD

When I met Patrick a few years back, I was more impressed with his humility than anything else. I had no idea who he was; I had no idea what he did for a living or where he spent his time when it came to ministry.

I remember someone whispering in my ear, 'Patrick is amazing and does way more than he will tell you. He's an OBE.' (I was unfamiliar with the term 'OBE' at the time.) But as Patrick and I began to talk, and he began to share his heart with me about his love for the lost and those on the fringes of society, I quickly realised not only what a wonderful man he was as a believer, but I was drawn to how visible his heart was for those who often get overlooked.

Following our initial meeting, I made sure I took a bit of time to go and see what Patrick was doing with XLP while I was in London. It was phenomenal. It was beautiful. And it looked like a place where Jesus would be hanging out. I loved walking around and seeing the places Patrick was overseeing, and I loved his team. But most of all I loved hearing the impact of what Patrick was giving his life too. Ministry is never easy, but ministry where young people are knifing each other and parents are losing children is heart-breaking. Watching the system fail in so many ways is exhausting. Some churches are already getting involved in local social action, others don't have the volunteers or resources. But Patrick's heart was in it.

Years later we connected again, this time over another

area which is often overlooked and full of stigma, yet perhaps the most important aspect of an individual's life: our mental health. If our mental health isn't good, then it's virtually impossible to become all we are meant to become this side of heaven. Our mental health matters. One's own emotional health (which also involves our spiritual as well as physical health) can't happen without honesty. Healing cannot take place without truth, and the truth does not come out if we don't feel that we have safe spaces in which to be truthful.

Patrick's new focus with Kintsugi Hope – a picture of God taking the parts of our lives where the enemy meant to destroy us and creating beauty within imperfection and brokenness – is not only full of hope, but I also believe, timely. Personally, when I feel that I am struggling, the Church tends to make me a bit nervous. *Will they accept me? Will they judge me? Will they allow me to be honest without the fear of reproof?*

I am sad to say, I have never felt these things with friends who don't know the Lord, or who don't attend church, but I've always had a bit of a fear of falling into the hands of the Church, as if I'm not quite safe. We say we want people to be honest, but when they are, it can actually frighten us. What people struggle with is real – it's not pretty, and it's often messy. But it's the truth of how hard life can be, the battle we live in, and the scarring of those battle wounds. This is not heaven – and until Christ comes again, the battle is real and the effects of battle are real. And sometimes we just don't know what to do with other people's struggles, let alone our own. To be truly vulnerable is scary for most people, but this is what the enemy feeds on, as he desires to silence us into bondage and to keep us isolated and alone. And the fear of rejection keeps many people in the Church silent.

That's why I believe this book is timely. It is needed. Sometimes we just need to hear from others who are working out their own salvation while continuing to deal with personal struggles. These pages don't shy away from the raw emotions of Patrick's own journey, as he pushes past fear so that others will feel safe in the knowledge that they are not alone; nor are they crazy because they have problems.

If you fear opening up or 'coming clean', I want to encourage you to take your time with these pages and know that despite perhaps feeling alone, you are not alone. The more we all share, the more healing can take place. When we find our voice, we find our freedom. *Honesty Over Silence* brings freedom just in reminding us that even at our worst, God is present. He desires not our perfection, but our trust.

Walking through London all those years ago, I remember looking down at Patrick's legs, knowing he was in pain (pre-surgery). During those hours together, what had the most impact on me was that in spite of pain, Patrick carried on. In pain, and in discouragement, he still made the choice to get up and do what God has called him to do. When we walked back to his office, I asked him about the pain in his legs, and he didn't sugarcoat it. He was in pain, and he was honest about it.

One of the greatest gifts we can give to each other is the truth about where we are at, and the reality of the struggles we carry. People don't identify with our strengths; they identify with our humanity. And the greatest story we have is how God is with us, and we can continue to say yes to Him, even in our broken state. Even when we don't see the healing or get the answers we have been waiting for, it is honesty before God and others that makes the most impact. Finding your voice is not only about finding freedom for yourself, but for the many who watch your life.

I am honoured to be a part of this and to applaud Patrick for sharing the hard stuff, breaking stigma and coming out the other side. I love how this book shows us that in spite of hardship, God never wastes anything. He can take the most broken parts of our lives and create unimaginable beauty. As you read this book, I hope and pray that you allow God to bring healing to the areas of your own life where you need Him most.

Christy Wimber

PART ONE

LEARNING TO LET GO

CHAPTER 1

LETTING GO OF THE PRETEND SMILE

When I wrote *When Faith Gets Shaken*, I was determined to be honest about my struggles.

After many years of excruciating pain in my knees, I had to have major limb reconstruction surgery. This involved breaking the fibula and tibia, severing the associated muscle and tissue, and having nine pins screwed into my leg (four of which went all the way through the leg and out the other side; the other five were screwed into the bone). These pins attached to a huge metal frame that circled around my leg, and were adjusted to help my bones set straight. Being in so much pain – and being fixed to such a huge frame – I had limited mobility, and my wife, Diane, had to clean the sites where the metal went into my leg to prevent infections. I wore the frame for six months and, even after it came off, there was still a long road to recovery.

Physically, the journey was tough – but in some ways the mental, emotional and spiritual journey was far tougher. I felt like I was running on empty; overwhelmed with anxiety, sometimes seething with anger, and desperately trying to find hope when everything looked bleak. I was anxiously trying to see where God was at work in it all, and in the other struggles we were dealing with – which included my dad having cancer, my daughter Keziah having a horrible condition called HSP (Henoch-Schönlein purpura), and Diane and I losing a baby in the early stages of pregnancy.

We were dealing with so much, and I was done with being one of those people who say everything is OK when it's not. Why do we do that? Why do we assume that people don't want to hear how we really are; they just want to hear that we're fine? Why do we think we have to present a perfect image to the world that says we're coping, no matter what is going on?

So the purpose of *When Faith Gets Shaken* was to be real and honest, but I was still hesitant. Despite my intentions, truthfully I wondered if people would judge me and question whether I was really a Christian if they knew the extent of my anxiety and doubt. Throughout the writing process I worried that I wouldn't find the right line between honesty and introspection, healthy disclosure and over-sharing. I didn't want to wallow in the things that had happened to me, well aware that I wasn't the only person facing challenging circumstances. But once the manuscript was submitted, there was no turning back. The book was published and my story – some of my most private thoughts and fears – was out in the world for anyone to read, for anyone to judge. I don't think I've ever felt so vulnerable.

Within weeks I started receiving emails and messages on social media, and the common theme seemed to be people saying, '*Me too!* I'm struggling as well; I've got pain and doubts and fears and I don't always know how to deal with them, particularly when I feel I should have faith.' I received messages from some of the most wonderful people going through desperate and heart-breaking situations. One in particular stuck out for me. A lady called Vivien wrote and said:

I loved my job as the manager of a busy pub. I felt needed, like I was making a difference in my community. I wore my busy-ness like a badge of honour, but one day it all came to an abrupt halt. My ankle collapsed, partly due to osteoarthritis, and I had replacement surgery to try to fix it. It never occurred to me that there would be any problems with the op or my recovery, and I fully expected to be bobbing back to work within the minimum six to eight weeks' recovery time. After all, I was a Christian and I had lots of prayer support from my church community, so why wouldn't everything be fine?

But everything went horribly wrong from the first moment. A nerve was accidentally severed during surgery, I developed multiple infections, and six weeks of plaster turned into five months in a wheelchair. I developed a blood clot in my lung, all the metalwork didn't bed in properly and, as I was on steroids, my bone didn't grow.

I was distraught. I felt guilty that I had let my prayer supporters down by not being healed; I felt robbed of an amazing testimony of healing and I dreaded people asking me how I was getting on. I began to have a sneaky feeling that maybe God didn't love me enough to heal me... maybe I wasn't even a Christian after all? I felt I had lost my identity; that I was useless and a burden. And then the well-meaning friends started with the 'I wonder why God hasn't healed you...' conversations, which hung in the air like accusations.

I kept a prayer diary during some of that time, and the pages are full of either woeful lament, or desperate attempts at self-motivation to kick-start my hope again. And in the midst of this kerfuffle, a wonderful friend sidled up to me in church one day, mightily apologetic, and thrust a copy of *When Faith Gets Shaken* into my hand, saying God told her I was to read it.

I didn't start off with very good grace (I was firmly attached to my pity puddle), but it felt like you [Patrick] had read my mind. I was jumping up and down (mentally at least!) saying, 'That's me – that's how I feel too!' It released torrents of tears, but gave me permission to express how I was feeling to friends and, more importantly, to God. It restored my relationship with Him.

Now, 17 months on, I am still in an air-cast, on crutches, and awaiting a consultant's decision as to whether I am to have the whole procedure done again or not. I still firmly believe in miraculous instant healings – I've been privileged to see them – but I now know that this situation is a far deeper source of loving healing and refining than just fixing a wonky ankle and spitting me back out into a crazy job again. I've come to see just how amazingly blessed I am to have been given this experience – the people I've met, the stories I've heard and shared, the things God has shown me – none of this would have happened otherwise. But it was the honesty of *When Faith Gets Shaken* that put me in the place of being able to receive all that God has for me, and for that, I am eternally grateful.

The circumstances may have been different in every story I heard, but nearly everyone said the same thing: 'I appreciate your honesty and vulnerability; now I can be honest and vulnerable too.'

I'm a big fan of Brené Brown, who has spent many years researching courage and vulnerability. She says:

> 'Vulnerability sounds like truth and feels like courage…
> Vulnerability is the birthplace of love, joy, courage,
> empathy and creativity. It is the source of hope, empathy,
> accountability and authenticity. If we want greater clarity
> in our purpose or deeper and more meaningful spiritual
> lives, vulnerability is the path.'[1]

It's the sort of quote that sounds brilliant – until we try to put it into practice! It's hard. We risk others judging us and even hurting us, but we have to be willing to share our imperfections if we are to become more human and more approachable. There's always a risk, but there's also the possibility that we will help someone else, and that they will show us love and acceptance – making us feel less alone too. I was totally humbled by the response to my vulnerability. It was healing for me to see people respond not with judgment but with love and understanding. I was so grateful that God had taken something so awful in my life and used it to help other people in their own pain.

ON THE ROAD

The next challenge for me was the idea of taking *When Faith Gets Shaken* on tour. I was filled with doubts about whether anyone would come; whether it would be helpful; whether it would look self-promoting. I spent far too much time worrying what people would think of me. Thankfully, I was working with the brilliant Andy Flanagan, a good friend of mine – a talented singer-songwriter who loves to use music to explore how we find hope in a broken world. The tour picked up the themes of the book, while Andy and I shared as honestly as possible about some of the challenges we'd faced, and how we found God in the midst of some very dark moments.

From both the book and the tour, I was astounded at how many people were willing to let their guard down and put aside their perfect smiles when they saw that we were willing to be real too. Every night, people came to share their stories: people who had cancer or who were seeing those they loved being ravaged by the disease; those with a myriad of mental health challenges – often that had plagued them for years; marriages that were breaking up; people who could only express their pain through self-harm; those dealing with domestic violence and abusive relatives; young people who told of failed suicide attempts and a lack of hope for the future. Faced with these heart-breaking situations, I wondered how much sharing my story would help but it turned out there was a power in breaking the silence – it allowed others to talk about their deepest pain too.

One of the most powerful points in the evening would always be when we challenged the idea that when we suffer, it's our fault. For me, that had been a huge struggle – as though I had somehow brought suffering on myself. I would describe a scene in the film *Good Will Hunting*, where Will, a troubled but gifted young man (played by Matt Damon), is meeting with his psychotherapist, Sean (played by Robin Williams). In the scene, Sean holds up the file detailing the years of abuse Will has suffered and says, 'It's not your fault.' Will shrugs it off, but Sean says again, 'It's not your fault.' He repeats and repeats the same line until Will breaks into sobs as the truth finally washes over him. He knew in his head he'd done nothing to deserve it, but his heart hadn't received the same message until that pivotal scene.

Do we struggle with that same truth? Do we consciously (or sub-consciously) think that we have somehow caused our own suffering because of our sin, because we misheard God, because we don't have enough faith or because we don't trust God enough? Sometimes we struggle to accept it's not our fault because our self-esteem has been so damaged that we believe, when things go wrong, that it must be down to us. At the heart of it, we're often questioning, 'Does God really love me?'

In the Church, we've often added to this by misquoting Scripture in saying, 'God won't give you more than you can bear.' The idea of this can cripple us when we feel that we can't cope. It was a phrase that was unhelpfully shared with me during the long process of my knee operations, and only made me feel angry and unloved. When someone tells you God wouldn't give you the burden if you couldn't handle it, you feel as though God can't know you at all – or that you are just failing some sort of weird test that He has set. It implies He's the one doling out the pain, and will push you right to your limit but then stop right before you crack.

The verse people are referring to when they say this is 1 Corinthians 10:13, which actually says God won't allow you to be *tempted* beyond what you can bear. The writer, Paul, was trying to show the Corinthians that God was with them when they were tempted, and would help them find a way to resist. We need to let go of this strange image of God measuring out how much pain we can deal with. This only confuses our understanding of who He is and how He relates to us in our suffering. I know people mean well when they say it. They're usually trying to find an encouragement in a painful situation and that can be difficult. But sometimes, rather than trying to find a spiritual explanation, it's better to just say, 'I'm sorry things are tough. I don't understand why you're going through all of this, but I am here for you and am I standing with you.'

We finished the *When Faith Gets Shaken* tour sessions by talking about the cross, and inviting people to write down on a sticky note someone or something – perhaps an issue or a memory – that they felt like they had been carrying for too long. There was then time and space for them to bring that note to the front and place it on the cross, symbolically saying, 'God, I need you to help me with this, I can't do it on my own.' Meanwhile, Andy would sing a song of lament based on Psalm 22 ('My God, my God, why have You forsaken me?'). It was such a moving experience to see row after row of people coming out of their seats and fixing some of their deepest pain and disappointment to the cross. The things people had been carrying were heart-breaking:

— I didn't say the right things to my son as he was dying of leukaemia.

— I fear that my past will catch up with me.

— My husband is paralysed from the neck down following an operation. I'm a single parent, carer, advocate and wife. I'm angry that it happened despite 24-hour prayer for him.

— I feel dead. School is making me so nervous.

— I just want to know... does God love me?

— Lord, I feel like I've become so distant from You. Please help me to find my way back.

— My sister is terminally ill with cancer of the liver and pancreas.

— My friend died when I took him out in my canoe. I couldn't save him.

— I feel like I am drowning in my own tears.

— I feel lonely.

— I feel guilty being pregnant when my best friend and her husband just lost their little girl.

— I feel like I will never be good enough.

THE ONGOING JOURNEY

Doing the tour made me realise this story wasn't over for me. I already knew that practically, in that I had another operation to come, which would bring with it many challenges – but, more than that, I had lots more to discover about how we walk through pain and suffering with God. That's how I've come to write this book. I want to explore some of the things we don't talk about very often in church; to look at the reality of trusting God through life's ups and downs; to think about how we can let go of our desire to be in control and our need to watch the clock, and instead trust God and His timing. I want to look into issues I have struggled with, knowing they are struggles for others too (such as anxiety and depression, and parenting a child with special needs). I want us to learn to recognise our negative thought patterns and be kinder to ourselves. I'm keen to explore the need for lament and the place for bringing all our questions, doubts, anger, pain, confusion and fear to God. We don't get to choose when darkness comes into our lives, and we will all face it sooner or later. The choice we have is whether or not we engage with the darkness, knowing that God meets us right there in our pain.

Before we can start the journey, first we need to know that it's OK to ask questions. It's an important part of lamenting (expressing our sorrow) and something we see repeatedly in the psalms (almost half of which are laments). David never held back in his honesty, and we frequently see other characters in the Bible questioning God too, trying to make sense of what He was doing and what His plan was. Despite knowing that,

I still feel guilty when I question God. Immediately a small voice says, 'You don't trust Him enough' – and I try and silence my questions, only to find they don't go away.

Some of the psalms that ask questions are described as 'psalms of disorientation', such as Psalm 13:

'How long, LORD? Will you forget me for ever?
How long will you hide your face from me?
How long must I wrestle with my thoughts
and day after day have sorrow in my heart?
How long will my enemy triumph over me?

Look on me and answer, LORD my God.
Give light to my eyes, or I will sleep in death,
and my enemy will say, "I have overcome him,"
and my foes will rejoice when I fall.

But I trust in your unfailing love;
my heart rejoices in your salvation.
I will sing the LORD's praise,
for he has been good to me.'

This psalm starts with a cry so raw that it almost sounds like a howl – but David is engaging with God in his pain, rather than turning his back on Him. There's such a deep honesty here as he questions God; he doesn't hold anything back in expressing his anger, disappointment and doubts. He seems to be saying, 'God, are you ignoring my pain?' Yet in all his confusion and hurt, he still acknowledges God as his Lord. We don't know what happens between verses 4 and 5, but David's words change from pouring out his pain to expressing his trust in God's unfailing love, offering his worship and promising that he will rejoice and remember God's goodness. That's where I want to try and stay – acknowledging who God is, even in the painful place.

How often do we give ourselves – and each other – space to journey honestly like this with God? Do we fear it? Lamentation is a part of the grieving process, and as Mark Yaconelli points out in his book *Disappointment, Doubt and Other Spiritual Gifts*, we're not always very good at dealing with our grief. He says:

> 'If I were to name the suffering that exists in the West, it is ungrieved grief. It is an unwillingness to admit, to name, to embrace the pain of loss. Many of the destructive practices of the Western world can be traced to a desire to distract ourselves from grief, what we're missing, what we've lost. Distracted from the reality of suffering, my heart hardens and I lose my capacity for compassion, I become less alive.'[2]

If we don't learn to grieve or lament properly, it's very hard to forgive properly. When we're hurt, we know the good Christian answer is that we must forgive – but if we try to rush that, we miss a vitally important part of the process. Grieving can bring freedom. It stops us from belittling the pain we're in and allows us to express it, giving it the care and attention that it's due, and from that place we can begin to move on.

INTO THE DARKNESS

From a very young age, we learn that darkness is bad and needs to be feared. It has negative connotations such as death, crime, depression, vampires and gangs – but as Barbara Brown Taylor points out in her book *Learning to Walk in the Dark*, we need darkness as much as we need light:

> 'Darkness is shorthand for anything that scares me – either because I am sure that I do not have the resources to survive it or because I don't want to find out... If I had my way, I would eliminate everything from chronic back pain to the fear of the devil from my life and the lives of those I love... At least I think I would. The problem is this: when, despite all my best efforts, the lights have gone off in my life... plunging me into the kind of darkness that turns my knees to water, nonetheless I have not died. The monsters have not dragged me out of bed and taken me back to their lair... Instead I have learned things in the dark that I could never have learned in the light, things that have saved my life over and over again, so that there is really only one logical conclusion. I need the darkness as much as I need the light.'[3]

One of my favourite games as a child was Hide and Seek, but playing in the daytime was boring. I liked playing at night – and even then, I'd find a dark spot (like a wardrobe) to wait until my dad came and found me. Even more exciting was when we'd go camping and would be outside at night in the pitch-black. I love that at first you can't see a thing, but as your eyes adjust, you become much more aware of your surroundings. Your other senses are heightened too; the sounds that appear frightening at first can be identified after a while, and the fear dissolves.

Instead of instinctively trying to run away from darkness, perhaps we need to learn to be comfortable there – to listen to the noises, to look up and see the stars, and to be reminded again that even in the darkest times in our lives, God has not abandoned us. Often things are the opposite of how they feel – and far from being distant, God is close and using the time to reveal more of His glory, to help us see the stars above us. Maybe there's more to discover in the darkness. Maybe it's time we stop trying to run, allow ourselves the time and space to adjust to the light, and ask God to be our guide as we walk in the darkness.

CHAPTER 2

LETTING GO OF ANXIETY

Despite having had limb reconstruction surgery once, the pain wasn't over. They can't operate on both legs at the same time, so I had to wait to recover from the first operation and then go back on the waiting list to have it all done again.

After being on the list for 18 months, I couldn't take it any longer. I made an appointment with the consultant and told him that, psychologically, I couldn't handle not knowing when the operation would happen. The weight of it – and the thought of the long recovery – hung over me every single day. It was difficult to plan anything at work or with the family because as soon as the operation was scheduled, we knew we'd have to clear our diaries for six to 12 months to allow for recovery. I couldn't see past it, and my anxiety shot through the roof. I lay in bed at night, desperately trying to distract myself, but I couldn't think of anything else. All the worst case scenarios of what could go wrong during and after the surgery went round and round in a never-ending loop in my head. I worried about my family, aware of the toll the last operation had taken on Diane and the kids. I worried for myself over the physical, emotional and mental exhaustion ahead. The first time, the operation nearly broke us in various ways, and I feared it would be the same (or even worse) the second time around.

When the consultant could see the impact the wait was having on me, and finally gave me a date for the second surgery, I had mixed emotions. It's incredibly rare to have this same procedure twice, especially due to a degenerative knee problem such as mine. The majority of similar cases are soldiers who have been injured in the line of duty, or people who've broken their leg in a motorbike accident. Most patients go through the hellish months of recovery only once, so they don't know what's in store. But I'd been here before, and knew exactly what I was letting myself in for. So, as grateful as I was that a date was set, I was scared. We had set in motion something over which I had no control. It wasn't so much like having butterflies in my stomach as it was feeling as if my whole body was in free-fall.

I wrote in my prayer journal that I felt like a drowning man, vulnerable, scared, and unsure of the future. I knew my anxiety was blowing everything out of proportion, and my thoughts were dominated by what *could* happen. Most of the conclusions I came to were, of course, negative, yet I still prayed that things could be different to the first time around. People had said to me back then that having time off work might not be a bad thing; that being largely immobile could give me time to reflect, rest and hear God's voice. (I had desperately wanted that to be the case, but found it very hard due to the high levels of pain and the impact of the lack of mobility.) Even with my previous experience in mind, I wanted God to bring something good out of this second recovery period. I knew I had no escape plan other than Him, and all I could do was pray honestly: 'If You don't come and rescue me, God, I will drown; if the ground doesn't appear under my feet, I will drown. I believe in You – help me in my unbelief.'

WORRY VS ANXIETY

We often think of worry and anxiety as being the same thing, but those who've experienced anxiety will know there's a huge difference. We all worry and, to a certain extent, it can be a helpful thing. For example, we may worry we won't get to an important meeting on time, and that encourages us to leave early and catch our train with time to spare – and so the worry goes. The perceived 'danger' has passed and the worry has no need to stick around. Anxiety, on the other hand, clings on in a much more insidious fashion. We feel anxious about every aspect of the meeting – from getting there to how it will go. Even after the meeting is over, the feeling doesn't leave as we're still anxious about how it went and what people thought of us. Worries are often temporary and prompt helpful actions to deal with the issue, whereas anxiety tends to be prolonged and takes us nowhere useful, just round and round in circles.

Worry is often something we experience in our minds, while anxiety can have an impact on our physical bodies. Anxiety puts the body in a heighted state of alertness, which can keep a person awake through the night; cause the heart to pound, cause dizziness, headaches and stomach upsets, and can result in constant fatigue, an inability to concentrate or a shortness of breath. While most people can go about their daily lives with worries running around their heads, anxiety can be all-consuming and completely debilitating, causing people to take time off from work and avoid social situations.

Anxiety can make a person hyper-aware of what others think. I particularly relate to this description of anxiety by Kirsten Corley:

> *'More than anything else anxiety is caring. It's never wanting to hurt someone's feelings. It's never wanting to do something wrong. More than anything, it's the want and the need to be accepted and liked. So you try too hard sometimes.'*[1]

If I have a problem, I want to sort it out instantly. If I have upset someone, I need to get it sorted straightaway as I hate the feeling of things being unresolved. I often try too hard; Diane says I will always get 100% for effort, but she wishes I would cut myself some slack and learn to relax. People with anxiety tend to take responsibility for everyone else's problems. Of course, it's good to take care of your friends – but we can be over-responsible, thinking their problems must somehow be our fault or trying too hard to solve things for them.

Because of all of these reasons, anxiety is exhausting – not only for the person dealing with it, but for those caring and supporting, especially when a person needs constant reassurance that everything will be OK. After my first operation, it wasn't the physical challenges that Diane found hard (helping me to the bathroom in the middle of the night, and so on), it was hearing my constant *what-if*s and having to keep saying, 'It may be difficult but we will get through this.' She would understandably get frustrated and say, 'Why can't you just let it go?' I wanted to, but my anxiety had a hold on me.

Anxiety can also take its toll on our relationship with God. I felt intense guilt for struggling with anxiety in the first place, telling myself that I should have been able to trust God more. It felt like admitting my doubts made me a bad person who lacked faith.

THE DRIPPING TAP

It would often be something really small that would throw me off track. I was so exhausted that things I could usually cope with became completely blown out of proportion. If I lost something important, I felt like a complete failure. I'd get cross at the kids, and then believe I was an awful parent. If someone at work wasn't happy or was upset by a decision I'd made, my conclusion was that I must be an awful boss. When we're already struggling, it's the constant *drip, drip, drip* of lots of small things that can really keep us down. My experience was that I would constantly get frustrated at my inability to deal with the pressures of life, and could never find enough space to recover from the latest incident. When I was younger, a fashionable idea in Christian circles was that the devil can knock you down, but he can never knock you out. Ultimately, there's truth in the fact that Jesus has won the final victory over evil – but I for one have occasionally felt pretty knocked out! The idea of just pushing through has never held much weight for me.

My anxiety was particularly linked to my children, especially our youngest daughter, Abigail, who has special needs. When she was very young, we went for various tests to explore some concerns with her physical health (which I'll talk more about in Chapter 10). As Abigail got older, she also had behavioural challenges. It took many years for the doctors to give us an actual diagnosis, and even then it was a vague one of 'complex special needs', as they couldn't define exactly what was wrong. We felt utterly worn down. Appointment after appointment; vague and partial 'possible' answers; year after year of our minds running riot trying to fill in the gaps left by inconclusive tests. And even with a diagnosis, it's not as if there's a medicine to neatly resolve things within a few weeks. We have to manage Abigail's needs constantly and get as much help as we can. Whenever Abigail has a meltdown, I find it easy to jump to the conclusion that it's my fault and that she is upset because I am doing something wrong. I beat myself up for not knowing how to help her and for not coping, and all that does is make me more exhausted – which in turn makes everything that much harder to deal with.

Instead of taking a sympathetic stance towards my own needs and exercising some self-compassion, I find it so much easier to do the opposite. I manage compassion towards others, but not always for myself. If Diane is cross with the kids, I don't think it's a big deal. If I get angry, I shout and then apologise – and while the kids move on very quickly, I can beat myself up for days.

OVERCOMING ANXIETY

Most self-help books will contain lots of helpful, practical tips, which often centre around things like slowing down, getting a good amount of exercise, cutting back on caffeine, trying relaxation exercises, music, meditation and therapy. During the second part of this book, we'll look in more detail at things that I've found helpful, such as self-compassion, being still/mindful, being loved, and being grateful. But first, I want to look at something we have to do before we think about any of that: facing up to what we're dealing with.

Before I could start to deal with my anxiety, there was something much deeper that had to happen first: I needed to accept what I was struggling with. You can't deal with what you don't first acknowledge, and that takes courage, vulnerability and humility. Archbishop Desmond Tutu believes that acceptance is actually the opposite to resignation and defeat. As an activist, he often challenges the systems that create poverty – but first he has to accept that they are there:

> 'We are meant to live in joy... this does not mean that life will be easy or painless. It means that we can turn our faces to the wind and accept that this is the storm we must pass through. We cannot succeed by denying what exists. The acceptance of reality is the only place from which change can begin.'[2]

I needed to accept what I was going through, and I needed to let go of the shame and embarrassment I felt about struggling with anxiety, and start to be honest about how I felt.

(That feels like a strange sentence to me, because when someone else is dealing with anxiety, I don't for one second think they should be embarrassed or ashamed but somehow, when we're the ones struggling, we can hold ourselves to a different standard.) I needed to show myself the sort of compassion that Jesus showed; He was always far more concerned about caring for the broken than looking at how they got that way.

We shouldn't be ashamed of our scars, because a scar is always a place of healing. We can't stop each other from feeling shame (as that's something a person has to individually choose), but we can share our own pain, and that in turn helps others to realise they don't need to be ashamed about theirs. Telling our stories helps others know that they are not on their own, and that is one of the most powerful antidotes to shame there is.

I think it's time that we not only stop feeling ashamed and embarrassed about our pain, but learn to celebrate the beauty of the struggles we've been through. I love the story of the Japanese emperor who broke his favourite pot and sent it halfway round the world to be mended. The best the experts could do was stick three metal staples round it, ruining how it looked – so the emperor asked some local artists to see what they could do. They mended the pot using molten gold as glue, so that instead of hiding the cracks, they made them into a beautiful feature. This is now known as the art of kintsugi (which means 'golden joinery' in Japanese), where pottery is repaired with seams of gold. The process of repair makes the object even more beautiful than it was prior to being broken. Instead of hiding the scars, kintsugi makes a feature of them.

POWER IN WEAKNESS

In 2 Corinthians 11:22–30, we see that the apostle Paul didn't deny what was going on in his life, but spoke about the time he'd spent in prison for the gospel, how he'd been flogged, lashed, shipwrecked and at risk of death. He'd been hungry and thirsty, naked and cold. In the following chapter, Paul describes his weakness as 'a thorn in my flesh' (2 Cor. 12:7). There's been so much debate about what that 'thorn' was – whether it was a physical illness or related to the persecution he suffered – but whatever it was, Paul says that three times he prayed for it to be taken away. The Corinthians reading his letter would probably have expected him to say, 'I prayed three times and it was on the third time that Jesus healed me' before he encouraged them to persevere in prayer. Instead, what they got was this:

'Three times I pleaded with the Lord to take it away from me. But he said to me, "My grace is sufficient for you, for my power is made perfect in weakness." Therefore I will boast all the more gladly about my weaknesses, so that Christ's power may rest on me. That is why, for Christ's sake, I delight in weaknesses, in insults, in hardships, in persecutions, in difficulties. For when I am weak, then I am strong.' **(2 Cor. 12:8–10)**

Paul didn't just confess his weaknesses, he *boasted* about them. He revelled in them because he knew that he didn't need to be strong – that's God's job. We are all broken, and part of us getting mended is being able to admit when we're not doing so well.

Part of the process of recovery is realising that healing doesn't happen overnight. It's a journey, and far from looking as good as new, we'll look like those cracked Japanese pots. The golden threads are what make us unique; they are a part of our history and our journey with God. These repairs take time, patience and gentleness from others and ourselves. In His incredible love, God will make something even more beautiful out of the broken parts of our lives – if we allow Him to.

We all have our reasons for not wanting to speak up about our brokenness. One of mine was that I felt it disqualified me. I thought people wanted to hear from leaders who were strong and courageous, constantly 'walking in the victory' and full of faith, no matter what obstacles they faced. What I've come to realise is that often the thing we think disqualifies us is actually what qualifies us to speak. People want honesty and integrity; they want to hear from people who are authentic. We are all broken, but owning our story is one way we step out of shame. I think we should model a different type of leadership, one where we lead well because of our vulnerability not despite it, showing that we are not afraid to be a weak human being who reveals a strong God.

TRUSTING THAT GOD WILL CATCH US

I love reading stories of people who trusted God and saw amazing things happen. One of my favourites is Henri Nouwen, a Dutch Catholic priest, professor, writer and theologian. After nearly two decades of teaching at academic institutions, including the University of Notre Dame, Yale Divinity School and Harvard Divinity School, Nouwen went on to work with mentally and physically handicapped people at the L'Arche Daybreak community in Richmond Hill, Ontario. In the later part of his life he devoted himself to community, intentional prayer, writing and, perhaps surprisingly, the trapeze.

Nouwen tells the story of how he sat and talked with Rodleigh, the leader of a troupe, about flying. Rodleigh told him that the key to the trapeze is that the person flying must have complete faith in the person who will catch them. While it's the person flying who gets the attention from onlookers, the real work belongs to the catcher. If the flyer tried to grab the catcher's wrists, the chances are he or she would break one or both of their bones:

> *"'The secret," Rodleigh said, "is that the flyer does nothing and the catcher does everything. When I fly to Joe, I have simply to stretch out my arms and hands and wait for him to catch me and pull me safely over the apron behind the catch bar... A flyer must fly, and a catcher must catch, and the flyer must trust, with outstretched arms, that his catcher will be there for him.'"*[3]

What an incredible picture. When I think about it, the people I trust the most are those I know love me the most. I trust Diane more than anyone, because she has seen the worst and best of me and her love has been consistent, no matter what. I'm a slow learner, so it's taking me a while to realise that the God who sent His Son to die for me is also worthy of my trust. There is no greater love than to sacrifice your child, but it's something He did willingly for us.

When it comes to trusting in God, part of my problem is allowing the fact that I am loved to actually sink in. I find it too easy to believe that God is cross with me, angry about my failings and shortcomings. As a parent, I helped each of my children to learn to walk by picking them up and putting them on their feet again each time they fell. I was never cross with them or even mildly annoyed that they'd fallen; I knew they were learning, and they just needed a helping hand to get back up and try again. I don't know why I still struggle to remember that God is even more patient than any human parent in this scenario. His patience and care is amazing. He's more than willing to help us up each time we stumble, to encourage us to take the next step when He can see the fear in our eyes from the last fall, and to hold us close when we've bumped our knee and just need a hug while the pain eases. It's too easy to picture God trying to give us a lecture, pointing out our mistakes and telling us how we could do better, rather than remembering He's a loving Dad, whose heart is moved each time His child is in pain.

Henri Nouwen says:

'Keep saying "God loves me, and God's love is enough". You have to choose the solid place over and over again and return to it after failure… trust that one day that love will have conquered enough of you that even the most fearful part will allow love to cast out fear.'[4]

CHAPTER 3

LETTING GO OF THE CLOCK

After surgery, I had to have blood tests and X-rays every week to check there was no infection. Every Monday morning, Diane and I would make the two-hour drive to King's College Hospital in London. I hated the journey as it's very hard to get comfortable with a frame (you're not allowed to have your leg down for long). I would sit in the back with my knee put up on pillows, but there was little we could do to avoid the pain every time we went over an uneven surface of road. Speed bumps were not my friend. The blood tests were straightforward enough; you took a numbered ticket so you could see where you were in the queue. Even though we had to wait, we knew what was going on and roughly how much longer it would be until we were seen. The X-rays, on the other hand, would drive me mad. I would register at reception, then try to find a seat among all the other patients waiting for X-rays, while Diane would try and find a stool to support my leg. Then we would wait. After an hour or so, Diane would think about heading off in search of coffee, hesitating in case we were close to being seen and she'd be out of the room when I was called – but no, she would return with two coffees in hand, and yet another hour would crawl by.

As we did this so regularly, we knew there would always be a long wait, yet each time we wondered if perhaps we'd been forgotten – especially when people who'd arrived after us were called and we would still be sitting there. Each time I'd think, *They've missed me; there's been a mistake. My name must have come off the list.* I'd get increasingly frustrated, hoping that I would be called without having to go to the desk, but eventually I'd make my way over and double-check they had my name down. Every week I was given the same reply: 'We are very busy today but you are still on the list, don't worry.' In other words: 'You haven't been forgotten. Even though it feels like you have. Even though it feels like everyone else is coming and going far quicker than you, your name is on the list and you just have to wait until it's your turn.'

Of course, eventually we would get called, but even after the X-rays, the day wasn't over. We would then have to wait to see the consultant to talk through the results, so the whole process of waiting would start again. Every time our consultant would appear around the corner of the waiting room with a file in his hand, we'd look up in hope, praying the file bore my name, our hesitant smiles saying, *Please pick us, don't forget us*, only to hear another patient's name being called. Four or five hours after arriving at the hospital, we'd be finished, ready to begin the two-hour journey home. I'm incredibly thankful for our National Health Service, but I don't think anyone could say that's a fun way to spend a Monday. Especially not every Monday for six months.

HAVE I BEEN FORGOTTEN?

We can often look at others around us who seem to always have the things we want – a story of miraculous healing, a happy relationship, a dream fulfilled – and we think, *Hang on God, what's wrong with me? I've been waiting for what feels like forever. I'm sick of waiting, why hasn't it happened for me yet? Have You forgotten me? Am I still in Your plans?* We might think we could've handled the waiting better if we knew just *when* the thing we longed for would happen. Friends who have been through periods of unemployment have often said to me, 'If I knew that in six months I would definitely get a job, I could handle those six months so much better. Instead of worrying, I would use the time positively to volunteer or do some of the things I've been meaning to do. Instead I just have to keep on trying job application after job application, interview after interview, never knowing which one might be the right one. Sometimes you start to think you'll never work again.'

I've also met many people in churches (particularly men and women in their fifties, but not exclusively so) who feel that God has overlooked them. In years gone by they had a dream, something they felt was from God, yet it hasn't been fulfilled. They are left frustrated, hurt and feeling abandoned. Feeling overlooked and forgotten are some of the hardest emotions to bear. As someone who has spent many years working with young people, I understand and even applaud the emphasis put in many churches on raising up the next generation. But in doing so, let's not do a disservice to the older generation who carry such maturity and wisdom. If you are in the over-fifty age group and feel like you have been overlooked, I'd love to encourage you (as someone just a little bit younger!) that your value is seen. I firmly believe that God wants many of you to pioneer again. You are not forgotten.

In his book *Dirty Glory*, Pete Greig says this:

> 'Most people pioneer at least once in their lives, when they're young and idealistic... But gradually the worries of life and the deceitfulness of wealth constrain the blood rush of youth. We tame the wild and call it wise. And if we're not careful, before we know it we find ourselves looking back on a particular year or programme or conference as the spiritual highlights of our lives. We shake our heads in amusement at the youthful naivety of it all, we tell stories again and again and reminisce about the unbridled passion and ambitions that once fired our pristine souls.'[1]

It's hard to hang on to hope when the years pass and things don't change in the way we want them to. I've known many people who have resigned themselves to the idea that things are never going to happen for them. After I got diagnosed with my degenerative knee condition, lots of people said they believed I would be healed – so I decided to get as much prayer as possible. I had heard stories of many miraculous healings and knew God was more than capable of making my knees as good as new, so I had hope that He would heal me. Each time I was offered prayer, I would dutifully accept – whether it was from a friend, in church, or at a festival of thousands. At first it was easy enough to say yes; when nothing changed, I could shrug it off and think maybe healing would come soon.

But time after time, when I received prayer but remained in pain, it began to take its toll. It wasn't so easy to keep smiling when the prayers dried up and nothing had happened.

It became harder to say yes to prayer, but still I would try. I would listen closely to stories of healing at festivals and hope that today would be the day I would finally have a story to tell too. Sometimes a friend would say they'd had a word with a famous speaker at a conference who was known to have seen hundreds of people healed. That speaker would kindly pray for me, but still – nothing. After a while it became emotionally exhausting. Hope began to feel dangerous to me. I couldn't muster the required energy and faith to get prayer because I couldn't handle the disappointment when I didn't get healed. It was easier not to put myself through it. I resigned myself to the fact that physical healing wasn't going to happen for me in the way I desperately wanted; two painful surgeries were inevitable.*

SMALL STEPS TO HEALING

Two weeks before my second surgery, Diane finished work to look after me. I felt awful that she had to give up her job, but we couldn't see any other way of making things work. She knew we had a rough six months or so ahead, and this was her small window of preparation before we were thrown back into the trauma of the operation and its recovery. Unfortunately, Diane didn't even have time to put the kettle on after work before the phone call came: our youngest daughter, Abigail, had fallen over at school and broken her leg, which would have to be in plaster for seven weeks. That meant two of us in the house were unable to walk unaided.

Because of Abigail's complex special needs, she gets very anxious about lots of things, and walking again after breaking her leg became one of them. You could see the fear in her eyes; she was terrified of what could happen if she used her leg again. We did all we could to convince her it was safe, but she wouldn't let go of the security of her Zimmer frame. We tried everything, even taking her to a private physiotherapist who taught her different ways of getting around. In a moment of desperation I offered to pay our eldest daughter, Keziah, a tenner if she could get Abigail walking. She left the room after an hour, screaming in frustration that nothing worked. Eventually I hit upon the ultimate bribe: if Abigail walked without her frame, we would get her a puppy. Diane was not impressed with this approach (and perhaps it wasn't my finest hour); nevertheless, we are now the proud owners of a border terrier called Georgi Joy.

It took four months for Abigail to walk properly again. No matter how much we pressed her before then, she wasn't having any of it. It was incredibly frustrating, but we had to learn to go at her pace. We've learned the hard way that pushing her will only make things worse. We are conditioned for a fast-paced life – we are in the results-driven business – but healing is a gradual process.

When Abigail was having her plaster off, I was on quite a cocktail of medication (mostly varying strengths of pain relief) to help me, post-op. There were so many meds that it got very confusing, not least of all because some tablets were only needed to control the side-effects caused by other tablets. The plan was to gradually reduce all the medication over time, and slowly wean myself off it. But one day I woke up with less pain, so I thought I'd try to go without the stronger painkillers. By lunchtime I was snappy; by mid-afternoon I had lost all control of my emotions. I started crying and couldn't stop. I was scared and confused, not knowing what was happening and fearing I was having a breakdown. All my frustrations and anxieties seemed to pile on top of me, reducing me to a crumpled mess on the floor. Fortunately, I have family members in the nursing profession, and when I described through my tears what was happening to me, they asked about my medication. They patiently explained I shouldn't have just stopped taking it all together; I needed to gradually reduce the dosage to save myself from that kind of reaction.

I so desperately wanted to be done, to move on to the next stage where I wasn't completely dependent on painkillers, but physically I wasn't there yet. I wanted to be strong emotionally, but I was still low. Physical and emotional healing take time, and the two are often linked. We want the quick fix, but that isn't always what's best for us. I am learning a lot through my slow healing. I still have the occasional uncomfortable and restless night, but also days when I wake up full of gratitude for the love of my family, church and friends. I am trying to fully commit myself to the gradual healing of me as a whole person, and not just my leg. Don't get me wrong – if the process speeds up in any way, you won't find me complaining – I'm just trying to remember that it's a process, and we need to learn to celebrate the small steps in life.

THE WAITING ROOM COMMUNITY

Despite my frustrations with all the hospital visits, one positive thing I've discovered is the sense of community that can be found in a waiting room. I've met many other people who also have had frames attached to their legs, and there's an instant camaraderie that's born out of the conversations you can't have with anyone else: 'How long has your frame been on? What pain control are you using? Have you had any pin-site infections?' We all share a smile over the number of people who ask, 'Do you take it off at night?' (It takes a team of trained medical staff to take it off in a long procedure usually done under general anaesthetic!) It's so good to discover you're not alone. It's the same when Diane and I talk to other parents of children with special needs; there's comfort and shared understanding about the frustrations and difficulties, as well as the immense joy and pleasure that kind of parenting experience can bring. It's often less obvious to tell if someone is struggling with anxiety, a challenging relationship or similar, but I can guarantee that whatever waiting room you are in, there are others going through the same thing. Talking to someone who understands can lead to some very deep and healing conversations.

Biblically, we're in good company in the waiting room too. Most of us know the story of Joseph, and how he went from being a slave, to a prisoner, to a national president. If he'd gone for careers advice as a teenager, saying he wanted to be a government official with a lot of power, I'm guessing no one would have suggested the route he took to get there. Being sold into slavery after annoying your brothers, being falsely accused of sexually assaulting your boss's wife and spending years in prison aren't the usual steps you would take. Even when there were signs of hope, like the cupbearer who promised he would remember Joseph after his release, Joseph had to wait two more years in a dingy prison cell. Do you ever wonder what went through his mind over those two years? I'm willing to bet there were times he gave up hope of things ever changing, thinking that was it; he would likely die in that place, forgotten and invisible.

In the New Testament, we read about Paul – the greatest apostle to the Gentiles – who was desperate to get to Rome, and then on to Spain, in order to preach the gospel. Could there be a more noble and divinely inspired dream? Yet he too spent two years in prison on false charges. Why didn't God do something? Surely Paul was the main man at this point; had God forgotten him or changed His plan? Had God forgotten Joseph as he sat in jail? How about David, who spent years waiting to see the fulfilment of God's promise that he would be king? It's impossible to say all that God was doing through these times of waiting. His ways are higher than our ways (Isa. 55:8–9) – or, as we could say instead, 'His ways are often very confusing for our earthly minds but He knows what He's doing.' One thing we do know is that God ultimately fulfilled His plans for Joseph, for Paul, for David, and they each went on to have powerful ministries. It's likely that God was dealing with their characters so they could handle all that was to come their way. Often we are so focused on the destination that we forget that God is more concerned with the state of our hearts as we journey towards it.

I believe God wants to make sure we are faithful in the hidden and the boring places, whether we feel trapped like Joseph in a prison that's not of our own making, are serving faithfully like David in a role that doesn't excite us at all, or frustrated like Paul when things stand in the way of our God-given dreams. Will we choose to keep looking to Him? Will we trust and allow Him to do what He wants to do in our hearts while we wait to see where He's taking us? Nicky Gumbel, vicar of Holy Trinity Brompton (HTB) in London, once put it like this:

'Joseph waited 13 years. Abraham waited 25 years. Moses waited 40 years. Jesus waited 30 years. If God makes you wait, [you] are in good company.'[2]

Who you become while you are waiting is as important as what you are waiting for. For me, times of waiting have often been when God has chosen to deal with issues in my heart, teaching me things I never would have learned if I'd got what I wanted straightaway. I can't always see the bigger picture, and I certainly can't see the future, but I do know that God is interested in who I am becoming far more than all my activity. He often reminds me that how I treat my wife and children is far more important than how polished a talk is for a conference; that He'd rather I get to know Him better than that I get the answers I'm looking for in my prayers. God is with me and much closer than I can imagine – it's just that I'm often too busy or distracted to recognise Him.

You may have heard the story of a guy called Joshua who decided to busk in a Washington DC metro station during morning rush hour. He played his violin for around 45 minutes and during that time, it's estimated that over a thousand people walked by. Hardly anyone stopped to appreciate his music – they were all too busy and had places to be. A few threw money his way without breaking their stride (he raised $32 in total, which some might say isn't too bad). But here's the thing: Joshua's surname is Bell, and he is one of the finest violinists in the world. Soon after, he played to a sell-out crowd in the city's best concert hall, and people paid through the nose to hear him perform on the very same violin – believed to be worth $3.5million. Bell's busking experiment had been to explore 'context, perception and priorities'. *The Washington Post* prefaced their article on the event with this simple, challenging question: 'In a banal setting at an inconvenient time, would beauty transcend?'[3]

I wonder if God sometimes feels like Joshua Bell did as people rushed past him, oblivious to the incredible beauty he was offering them. What God has to say to us is so precious, and yet we're often too busy to listen. How many times do we come to pray with our hands full of our own agendas and timetables – too full to receive what He has to give us? How many times do we plan how we think things need to work out and then ask God to get on board with our timings, rather than trusting His ways? Waiting reminds us we are not in control, and we can't command things to happen on a schedule that suits us. Sometimes we need to let go of our own plans and ideas. We need to stop rushing and just wait a while, listening to God's whisper.

GOING DEEPER

With the advantage of hindsight, I now know that some of my times of waiting have actually been times of preparation, and have brought a greater depth to my faith. So, rather than losing hope and resigning myself to things staying the same (as I may be tempted to do when the road ahead is long), I want to trust the character of God. Vaclav Havel, the former President of the Czech Republic, once said: 'Hope is not the conviction that something will turn out well, but the certainty that something makes sense, regardless of how it turns out.' We can't always understand the ways of God, but we can trust that He is working for our good, regardless of how our circumstances appear (Rom. 8:28).

God has always wanted to be with His people, pursuing them, longing for a relationship with them, and fundamental to this relationship is that we trust Him. He won't explain all the mysteries of life to us now – the limited capacity of the human brain wouldn't have a hope of understanding – so we need to trust Him in the unanswered questions. We choose to trust despite our frustrations. We celebrate His goodness even when we're in pain. We believe He is teaching and guiding us even when it feels like He's forgotten us.

I don't enjoy suffering at all, but I grudgingly admit that it has been my best teacher, and it's taught me things I am not sure I could have learned any other way. When we suffer and when we wait, our perspective changes. We rethink where we want to invest our time, we become more understanding and less judgmental, we grow in compassion (our awareness of our own fragility helps us understand the fragility of others), we become kinder, softer and more full of grace. Because of the things I've been through, my faith has become less of a set of black and white beliefs, or a list of religious boxes I have to tick each day. It's become more about recognising God, and seeing Him moving in everyday life. God doesn't solely exist in our churches or at our large festivals and events, as wonderful as some of them are. He's in the kindness of my Nan, who had so little but wouldn't let me leave her house without stuffing a fiver in my hand. He's present in the laughter shared with a fellow patient in the waiting room. He's in the people I meet who have been through so much more than I can imagine, yet reflect God in ways that are genuine and pure. They are not perfect, but have somehow let go of bitterness and allowed God into their pain and unanswered questions.

SEASONS CHANGE

Sometimes it can feel like the waiting will never end, but seasons always change. Moving from London to the countryside has really brought home to me how the change in seasons affects everything: the ground, the trees, the skyline. Each season is defined and brings a marked change from the previous one. In London, it was difficult to notice any difference between seasons (they all brought rain!).

Life's seasons can drag on, and we can start to believe they will last forever. 'How long, oh Lord?' said the psalmist. 'How long until this season of pain passes and life is good again?' But even if a particular season lasts for years, the truth is that it *will* eventually shift. We might feel like we've been buried underground and forgotten, when God has actually planted us. It may take a long time for any evidence of growth to be seen above the surface, but seeds germinate best in darkness. Though those first few spurts of growth are hidden from sight, they are key to the long-term health and growth of the plant. The seed stays put, and eventually its growth is visible. Likewise, let's hold onto the fact that even when we feel like we're abandoned in the darkness, God is at work.

For those of us who are Christians, we are all waiting for the ultimate change in season: Christ's return. Then there will be a new heaven and new earth where all suffering, pain, injustice and inequality will be gone. God moved into our neighbourhood many years ago and has promised to come back, bringing complete restoration of all things. We will see the end of fear, anxiety, suffering, sickness and disease, but until that time we wait, working with Him to bring about His purposes in the here and now, trusting that He will come.

*As a side note, it took my psychologist to point out to me that I wasn't obligated to go for prayer every single time it was offered. I put pressure on myself that it was the 'right thing to do', when it would have been kinder to myself to say yes only when I felt it was right, not just because it had been offered.

CHAPTER 4

LETTING GO OF THE STIGMA

'You've got a migraine? Surely it's mind over matter. Think happy thoughts and you'll be fine.'

'Broken your leg? It's all in your head. Stop thinking so much and just shake it off!'

'Cancer? Could be worse – chin up.'

We would never talk to someone with a physical ailment like this, and yet anyone who has suffered with a mental health issue is likely to have been told it's all in their head, or that they should be able to 'get over it'. Depression and anxiety aren't things we can pull ourselves together over. It's not a person's fault, and it's not something they can control.

As a society we're more comfortable talking about and looking after our physical health than our mental health, but we haven't always known so much about caring for our bodies. Years ago, people didn't know that brushing your teeth keeps them from going rotten and falling out, or that washing daily is a good idea (the Anglo-Saxons thought the Vikings spent far too much time bathing because they did it once a week!). We have learnt a lot over time about physical health, in terms of prevention, treatment and cure. But in the area of mental health, we've still got a long way to go. While most of us know what to do if we get a headache or a minor cut, and it's usually fairly obvious when we need to call an ambulance, few of us seem to know how to take care of the emotional and mental needs of ourselves and others. Perhaps if we spent as much time caring for our mental health as our physical health, we would be much happier as a society.

THE HIGHLIGHTS REEL

When my anxiety started to get out of control, it was easiest for me to point to my upcoming surgery as the sole source of my problems. However, the truth was the anxiety was about much more than just one thing. From the outside, you might have missed it altogether. Things were really thriving at XLP, the charity I founded to work with young people in London. We were at a very exciting time, with two visits from the Duke and Duchess of Cambridge in just one year. It was a huge privilege to introduce them to some of the young people we work with, and share stories of how XLP's mentoring project was now happening all over the country. They listened to some of the amazing young people sing who have come through the XLP arts programme, and then afterwards hosted a reception for business leaders.

As you can imagine, a lot of work goes on to make sure everything runs smoothly for a 90-minute royal visit. While William and Catherine are actually very easy to be around and very good at putting others at ease, the media circus that surrounds them is not. We stepped outside the doors of the church and were greeted by a wall of photographers, cameras flashing constantly as we paused for pictures. I have no idea how they live like that. Photos of the XLP team and young people with the royal couple went everywhere, flooding social media, being shared hundreds of times. Numerous newspaper articles were written, and the BBC featured the visit on the six o'clock news. To anyone watching, XLP was doing really well. And while a royal visit is an exciting occasion and well worth celebrating, it's also just part of the highlights reel – it doesn't indicate what's going on behind the scenes. You can look at hundreds of photos of me standing beside the future King of England, and seeming perfectly confident in the accompanying TV and radio interviews – but inside, I was a very frightened individual struggling with anxiety. It wasn't meeting royalty that made me nervous, nor was it the media. I couldn't shake my fears over the uncertainty around my health and my future.

I knew we needed to maximise the opportunities that the royal visit brought to XLP. Having such high-profile interest is incredibly helpful when you're trying to raise money for a charity and, like lots of similar organisations, XLP really needed the money. I threw myself into the task full-throttle, knowing my operation was coming up and that I didn't have any time to waste. I tried to get to see as many potential funders as possible and was driving myself very hard, working long days and late nights. Exhausted, I frequently snapped at Diane and the kids and would then get frustrated with myself because I knew they had done nothing wrong.

There was a lot going on for us as a family too. We had recently moved house from London, which had been my home for 23 years, to the suburbs where Diane and I had grown up. The cultural shift was huge, and I was struggling to get my head around our new life compared to the London busyness that I had grown so accustomed to. Our teenage daughter was also finding the transition difficult and was particularly struggling with friendships, being 'the new kid' at school. Diane and I knew this was the right move for us as a family, but that didn't stop us feeling guilty when we saw Keziah having such a hard time. I was overtired, anxious, feeling guilty about Keziah, not coping with change, and finding the uncertainty around Abigail's health and behaviour difficult to cope with.

THE BLACK DOG OF DEPRESSION

Diane urged me to go on anti-depressants and get some help for my anxiety. It was an odd thing: even though I had advised many people over the years to seek medical help in such situations and not to feel ashamed of it, I somehow felt that I should soldier on and find a way to get through it. There can be a fine line between anxiety and depression, and I honestly couldn't tell if I was depressed, anxious, or both. Some days I felt a bit brighter and would think, *Great, I'm over that now*, and then for no fathomable reason I would wake up the next morning feeling like I had been consumed by a dark cloud. A familiar feeling of falling would come over me. My mind would be flooded with the *should*s, the *must*s, the *ought*s that told me I was failing.

'I *should* be able to cope – what's wrong with me?'

'I've got a family to look after, a team to lead and a job

I'm passionate about – I *must* pull myself together or I'll let everyone down.'

'I know that God loves me and is in control despite how things feel – I *ought* to be stronger, get a grip and spend more time praying. I am obviously not leaning on God enough.'

I sometimes wonder who is setting the standards we think we need to live by.

As hard as I tried, I couldn't seem to control how I was feeling. I tried some of the things that usually help when you're feeling a little bit low: I forced myself to walk the dog, go to the gym, and list some of the things I was grateful for, but nothing changed. It wasn't just a bad day that I'd soon get over, it was something much worse.

Depression is often likened to a dark cloud that hangs over you, or a 'black dog' that follows you around. I saw a video online, produced by the World Health Organisation, which describes the visits of the 'black dog'.[1] There is no reason why he visits, but when he's there, he colours everything else in the world. I could relate to so much of what the video said: how things that used to bring me pleasure no longer did, that my appetite was ruined and my ability to concentrate was shot. The 'black dog' stole my confidence, left me worried that I would be judged, and made me irritable and difficult to be around.

There's an ocean of difference between having a day where you feel down, and having depression. It's not even about being sad – depression can leave you completely devoid of feeling, and totally isolated. On my worst days, I thought everyone would be better off if I wasn't here. I told myself they would miss me but they would get over it in time… but then I would feel overwhelmed with guilt. I knew it wasn't true, but the thoughts really scared me.

I'm a self-starter, so I'd read all the self-help books. The real challenge was actually asking for help. I felt that if I went to the doctors, I would somehow be letting everyone down. No one was telling me that, but it's the conclusion I came to. I also felt uncomfortable with the focus being on me. I like talking about the bigger issues of injustice and inequality in the world and seeking out solutions, so all this talking about my personal feelings felt really self-indulgent. Over the years, I have come across people suffering through some of the hardest circumstances imaginable and I thought that if they didn't get depressed with all they'd faced, then I had no right to. Of course, that kind of thinking doesn't help. It's like telling yourself you've got no right to have a stomach pain – it doesn't make it go away.

Church can be a lonely place if you suffer from depression or another mental health condition. People often think that knowing Jesus should mean we're never depressed, but it doesn't work that way. Research by the mental health charity Mind says that one in four people in the UK will suffer from a mental health problem each year,[2] and one in six report experiencing something like anxiety and depression each week. That means each of us is likely to know someone who has it *now*, and multiple people who will. Sadly, being a Christian isn't an inoculation. Making Christians feel as though they should have some kind of immunity to depression only adds to the feeling of shame. The most common thing

I hear from people who are depressed – and something I struggled with too – is thinking, *It's my own fault.* The thought replays over and over and over again, and when we feel ashamed, it's that much harder to seek help or confide in anyone.

One of the things that makes depression so hard is that sufferers frequently question whether they are really ill or not. The Blurt Foundation, a social enterprise dedicated to helping those affected by depression, wrote a blog post called 'Ten Lies Depression Tells Us',[3] and it really made me think, *Wow! That's me!* Here's what they said:

Depression tries to convince us that we are not actually ill.

Depression tells us that everything is our fault.

Depression tells us that nobody cares about us or likes us.

Depression tells us that we're not good enough.

Depression tells us we don't deserve things.

Depression tells us that we're a bad person.

Depressions tells us to be quiet.

Depression tell us that we're a burden.

Depression tells us that we don't deserve help and support.

Depression tells us there is no hope.

This last lie is one of the most painful, and it is a *lie*. There *is* hope. If you feel like this, you are not alone and you are not a bad person.

JESUS, STIGMA AND OPPRESSION

Jesus always challenged stigma and oppression, but in a way that people didn't expect. Some of my favourite verses in the whole of the Bible are when Jesus stood up in His home synagogue, opened the scroll at Isaiah 61 and read this:

> 'The Spirit of the Lord is on me,
> because he has anointed me
> to proclaim good news to the poor.
> He has sent me to proclaim freedom for the prisoners
> and recovery of sight for the blind,
> to set the oppressed free,
> to proclaim the year of the Lord's favour.'
> **(Luke 4:18–19)**

Oppression can be defined as the feeling of being heavily burdened, mentally or physically, by some kind of trouble or adversity. Jesus made it His mission to set the oppressed free, and He always seemed to be drawn to those who felt stigmatised, the downtrodden, and those who felt worthless. He showed great mercy and compassion to those who didn't believe they were worthy of love or acceptance from anyone, let alone God.

Jesus stopped to eat with the tax collector Zacchaeus (Luke 19), who would have been seen as a traitor in the eyes of the Jewish people for exploiting those who were already poor. Sharing a meal was something you did with close friends and family, so Jesus inviting Zacchaeus to dinner was like a seal of approval for this man utterly despised by his community. In John 4, we see Jesus drinking water at the well with a Samaritan woman. Not only did Jewish men not interact with Jewish women in such circumstances, this woman was from a group of people the Jews didn't mix with at all. When Jesus spoke to her about her five husbands, He didn't disgrace her as some may have expected; He treated her with dignity and respect, only concerned with her finding freedom from her sin and shame. He knew the emotional rollercoaster she had been on; while others just judged her for what they could see on the surface, Jesus could see the bigger picture. Radically changed by her encounter with Jesus that day, she ran back to her community and said, 'Come see a man who told me everything I've ever done' (John 4:29). Commenting on this story, Christy Wimber says:

> 'Imagine the scars on this Samaritan woman. Imagine what she had to push through in order to show herself to those who had rejected her before. That had to take a lot of guts to risk rejection again, and with the same people, yet she did it anyway. The power of her encounter with Jesus was more powerful than the pain she had lived with all those years. The risk she took following that encounter impacted so many. You need to know people relate to your scars. People need to see examples of those who made it through difficult and painful times. The Samaritan woman led so many to Christ not because of her perfection, but her ability to share her story. Don't hide your story, don't hide your scars.'[4]

In Jesus' day, different people were stigmatised – 'traitors' like Zacchaeus, outcasts like the woman at the well, and those who were 'unclean', like the woman with chronic bleeding, and those with leprosy. One of the most prevalent types of social stigma today is around mental health challenges. We need to get to a place where people feel no more ashamed for having depression, anxiety or any other mental health concern, than they do having a cold or a broken leg.

When the news broke in 2013 that Rick and Kay Warren's son, Matthew, had taken his own life after many years battling depression, there was a huge sense of shock. Of course, there was the shock of someone so young dying and in such a tragic way – but there also seemed to be a sense of, 'How could this happen to such a high-profile Christian couple who lead a mega-church?' It's as though somewhere in our subconscious we think that, if you're following Jesus, surely you're immune. Rick and Kay gave an incredibly moving and insightful interview at the HTB Leadership Conference the year after they lost Matthew, where Rick said this:

> 'It is not a sin to be sick. Your illness is not your identity and your chemistry is not your character… Everything in this world is broken because of sin… So why is it that, if my liver doesn't work perfectly, I take a pill for it and there's no shame in that; if my heart doesn't work perfectly, I take a pill for it and there's no shame in that; if my lungs don't work perfectly, I take a pill for that and there's no shame in that; so why is it that if my brain doesn't work perfectly and I take a pill for that, I'm supposed to hide that?'[5]

One of the things that struck me most about this interview was that Rick and Kay talked so much about their son's strength. Matthew struggled from when he was a child, and had tried all the doctors and prayer that a person could get. His parents didn't see him as weak for having been depressed; they understood that to continue living under the cloud of depression for 27 years took great courage. Kay explained that some of the most courageous people are the ones who live with strong depression year after year after year, but who get up day after day after day, putting one foot in front of the other and trusting God even in darkest times. She said this:

> 'Our son was a believer in Jesus Christ but struggled so deeply with profound depression. And as I've talked to thousands of people since his death I hear from depressed Christians, and many of them feel ashamed because they come to their church and their church just tells them... to pray a little bit more, read their Bible just a little bit more, they've got sin they need to confess... Or they're minimised... One of the things the Church needs to do is recognise the value of people who have a mental illness or depression – what they bring and what they teach us about really walking with God when it doesn't ever feel good.'[6]

This seems to be a perspective adopted by many others too. In his book *Depressive Illness: The Curse of the Strong*, Dr Tim Cantopher writes:

> 'Normally, in a psychiatric assessment, one is expected to make enquiries about aspects of the patient's personality. I never bother, because it is nearly always the same. He or she

will have the following personality characteristics: (moral) strength, reliability, diligence, strong conscience, strong sense of responsibility, a tendency to focus on the needs of others before one's own, sensitivity, vulnerable to criticism, self-esteem dependent on the evaluation of others.'[7]

To me, this sounds like the type of person you would want as your best friend!

THE DEPRESSION HALL OF FAME

I find it so helpful that Cantopher also mentions a long list of people who have suffered at the hands of depression, including Oliver Cromwell, Abraham Lincoln, Isaac Newton, Vincent Van Gogh and Winston Churchill. After nearly every When Faith Gets Shaken talk, at least one person comes to ask for the above list – sometimes for themselves, but often to show family members to help them explain that their mental health issues aren't a sign of weakness.

We take great comfort and great inspiration from the saints who have gone before us and seen God do great things. What we don't always hear are how many of them suffered with mental health challenges. I have long known that Mother Teresa went through very dark nights of depression, but only recently learned more about Hudson Taylor. I had heard him mentioned in many sermons and knew him as the man who brought Christ to China, founding the largest mission there. But I was surprised to read that, though Hudson Taylor was ministering in the nineteenth century, he dealt with many of the challenges we face today. He struggled with self-doubt, anxiety, church politics, problems between the English office and the Chinese office, and he also faced a large amount of personal tragedy. Three of his children died, as did his first wife, Maria. He then married Jennie, and when she gave birth to one of their children, he was so unwell with a bad back that he could only lift himself up from his bed with the aid of a rope to see the baby. They also suffered the heartbreak of having stillborn twins.

As Hudson Taylor pioneered his work in China he was met with serious opposition. Many Chinese missionaries were murdered, and for the first part of his ministry, he struggled with anxiety and could behave very irrationally. In his book about Hudson Taylor's life, Steer writes:

'He began to ask himself a series of questions: is there no rescue? Must it be thus to the end – constant conflict and, instead of victory, too often defeat? He hated himself and hated his sin and would cry out "Abba Father".'[8]

The turning point came when he received a letter from his friend John McCarthy. He realised from the content of the letter that what he needed to understand was that the work was God's, not his. He commented: 'I have striven in vain to rest in him. I'll strive no more. For He has promised to abide with me – never to leave me, never to fail me.'[9] This was a major breakthrough for him, and he didn't struggle with anxiety again in the same way.

McCarthy's letter seemed to be a significant moment in

Hudson Taylor's, life but this doesn't mean that everyone's anxiety has the same root. From my experience, the reasons and treatments for anxiety are different for different people, and rarely does anxiety come on its own – it is often related to something else. The lesson here is not that all we need to do is trust God and get on with it. We are not God. We are not in control of all things. So why do we sometimes still act as though we are, and as though all the responsibility sits with us? Many of us whose strength is taking responsibility for things will find that our weakness is taking too much responsibility. There comes a point where we have to say, 'God, this is yours. Unless You build the house, we labour in vain' (Psa. 127:1).

ASKING FOR HELP

I finally decided I needed to go to the doctors. I just wasn't coping. I found myself crying for no reason, or struggling to hold it together. Having read the 'Ten Lies Depression Tells Us' blog I mentioned earlier, I knew I was taking things far too personally and often feeling misunderstood. In their book *Insight into Depression*, Chris Ledger and Wendy Bray explain it like this:

> *Having a sensitive character, or a spirit, which readily responds to the needs of others, is a wonderful gift. But the flipside of that gift is that we are vulnerable to the thoughtlessness, rudeness, spite and bad temper of others. It isn't enough to "toughen up" or "develop a thicker skin".*

Criticism can hurt – and hurt deeply. We may feel trampled on, wounded and rejected. If that hurt remains, unhealed and barely hidden or if it is inadvertently touched upon, it can lead to depression.[10]

Someone once messaged me out of the blue, saying they'd had a dream about me and the heart of it was that my anxiety and depression were a by-product of the compassionate heart God has given me. They said, 'You see a problem, it hurts, and you have to do something about it. When fixing the problems is a problem, you hurt. Don't wish the anguish away. Manage it and lean hard on the Holy Spirit. Look at Job, Elijah, and David – all men with hearts after God and all men who suffered in a similar way.' This was so encouraging – it helped me to put into context some of what I was dealing with, and be reminded that anxiety and depression are often caused by caring too much.

I still felt nervous sitting in the doctor's surgery, and I'm not sure why, but even writing about it gives me the same anxiety in the pit of my stomach. I went through the list in my mind of why I thought there was something wrong with me. I thought it was something I had to prove because there wasn't a physical symptom for the doctor to poke and prod. Thankfully, that was entirely unnecessary. He understood straightaway what I was trying to say and how hard it was for me to say it. We talked about some of the practical things I could do (carry on with my counselling, keep active, watch my diet, cut down on caffeine, etc), but he also suggested I try medication. I felt a mixture of relief and shame. I didn't want anyone to know, but I knew I had to let go of that feeling. I'm not saying that people on anti-depressants should have to broadcast it to the whole world – it's OK to keep it private – but I didn't want to hold back because of a false sense of shame. I wanted to write about it here so that anyone reading this book would know that it's OK not to be OK. It's OK to ask for help. It's OK to need medication for mental as well as physical health.

God doesn't condemn us for feeling like this. He wants what's best for us, so if that means taking medication, then we should be free to do that. That said, medication isn't always the answer to everything. Sometimes there are underlying issues to depression that would really benefit from counselling and additional support; sometimes we need to think about lifestyle factors such as diet and alcohol consumption. However, many find that anti-depressants help them get to a place of being able to look at those other issues, and they can be incredibly helpful.

It might take several attempts to find a medication that works, and sometimes people give up after experiencing negative side-effects. For two weeks I had a very bad headache, which the doctors said was normal, but I did start to feel my mood shift and that was a huge encouragement when I knew it could take up to six weeks to feel the benefit of the tablets. Before taking anti-depressants, I had started to believe that there was no way back – and had felt so much shame that I hadn't 'prayed my way back' to health. But as the bleakness began to recede, I began to see hope again. I still have a long way to go, but I'm so grateful that Diane encouraged me to go to the doctors. My depression was impacting her and the children, and taking medication was part of my commitment to be the best husband and dad that I could be. I hope you have someone in your life who can help you make the same decision, if you need to. If not, let me be that person. Let go of any shame that's stopping you and go to the doctors. They will understand. They can help you. And things can get better.

ALAN AND JACKIE'S STORY

We were travelling between venues on a When Faith Gets Shaken tour when we stopped for a coffee at The Old Bakery Tearoom in Stow-on-the-Wold, a beautiful place in Gloucestershire. It was there that we met Alan and Jackie Slough in the tearoom they own and run. We didn't realise they were Christians until we got chatting, and it turned out that Jackie had read *When Faith Gets Shaken*. She began to tell me their story, and I was incredibly moved and taken aback by their integrity, honesty and love for Jesus. The tearoom had a lovely atmosphere and I knew they were special people. Their story has had a huge impact on me and on many others, so I invited them to share it with you.

A word of warning: you may well find what they have to say incredibly painful, but Alan and Jackie have shown me that people can go through some of the worst things life could possibly throw at you, and still come out with hope, believing and trusting that God is good, and with a passion to help other people in their pain.

When we met in 1980, we shared a common dislike of religion. Our experiences of church had been of cold buildings, dull services, and a sense that you only went because it was what you *should* do, not because there was life and joy to be found in faith. We found it nauseating that so many religious people weren't real about how they were feeling. Pain was hidden behind fake smiles when life was hard, and Christian platitudes were frequently rolled out, saying everything is fine when that's actually far from the truth.

But despite that, when it came to discussing where we wanted to get married, we picked my (Jackie's) village church, and when our boys came along (James in 1984 and Tom in 1987), we wanted to get them christened – it was what you did. It wasn't until 1999 when a friend sent us a handwritten invitation to an Alpha course that we set foot inside a church in order to actually understand who God is. Initially we'd thought we'd go to prove these Christians wrong – but we soon realised that God was not only real, but wanted to have a relationship with us. The change in us was so dramatic that James and Tom both decided they wanted to do the course the following year and became Christians too. Our pastor said it was the first time he'd baptised four members of the same family within nine months!

Our life as a family began to revolve around church, and we threw ourselves into serving in any way that we could. James and Tom were the only two young people of their age in the church. They were typical brothers who fought and competed with one another. James worked hard at school, while Tom seemed to breeze through everything, particularly excelling at creative writing (even at junior school, his poetry and stories won him prizes). They both got good grades, but while James worked his socks off for his, Tom would do his homework on the bus and still get top grades (which understandably riled his brother).

Tom was bullied at times, both verbally and physically, but we weren't sure why. Even when he was a small boy, we remember other kids pushing him over for no reason – he just seemed to attract the attention of bullies. His teachers seemed reluctant to get involved, and for the most part it didn't seem too serious. But one evening, when we asked about his day, he said, 'It was fine, aside from thinking about suicide.' We were surprised, and though we tried to talk to him about it he shrugged it off and never mentioned it again, so we put it down to being one of those odd things that kids say.

Tom found a good group of friends when he got to secondary school, and though there wasn't anyone his age at church, he seemed passionate about his faith and was happy to share it with others. One of his history lessons turned into a debate about faith and Tom held court, happy to speak up for what he believed in. Of course, he was also experimenting with other things too – falling in and out of love with girls, starting to drink, going to parties – but, like most parents, we didn't know all that was going on, and nothing seemed out of the ordinary in his behaviour. To us he presented a happy and healthy person. It was only towards the end of his short life that we started to really worry about him.

Tom had always been a real chatterbox, but after his sixteenth birthday he suddenly became much quieter, choosing to spend lots of time in his room on his own listening to Nirvana on repeat. It's not unusual for teenagers to withdraw into themselves and James had gone through something similar, so we put it down to his age rather than to depression. We didn't like the music he listened to. It seemed so dark, and when we would go into his room there was often a strange atmosphere; a heaviness you couldn't quite put your finger on. Tom's healthy appetite seemed to lessen, and we later found out he was secretly drinking alone in his room (he watered down our brandy and other drinks so we wouldn't notice what was missing). Sometimes he would show us a poem he'd written that spoke of the pain and turmoil inside, but when we tried to talk to him about it, he found it too difficult to express. Writing was his release and his way of dealing with his emotions – as we discovered in the many more poems and journal entries we found after his death.

One night in December 2003, Tom came home drunk. Despite him running upstairs to avoid us, we could hear him being violently sick. We immediately went to check on him, and he said his drink had been spiked while he was out with friends. We'd never seem him drunk before and he was always well-behaved, so we believed him and called an ambulance. A kind paramedic took care of him and, outside of our hearing, got him to confess that he'd actually drunk a range of strong spirits, and after a check-up he was back to normal the next day.

One strange thing we noticed before school one morning was that Tom had red marks around his neck. We asked him about it, and he said they were caused by the chain he wore with a cross on it. He explained that he'd slept in it, and must have been at an awkward angle because the necklace left indents. We questioned it again when the marks were still there hours later, but he stuck to his story. We later found out those marks were from where he'd put a ligature around his neck: his first attempt to commit suicide.

A few weeks later we had a wonderful family Christmas – we all said it was the best one we could remember. James and Tom had recently begun to bond as friends as well as brothers, and they enjoyed each other's company in a way that made things easier all round. We went to church, opened presents, ate a huge Christmas dinner and relaxed in front of the usual seasonal television.

On Friday 30 January 2004, Tom was up early for school. We usually had to pester him to get ready, but he was up before either of us. Nothing else seemed unusual; he said goodbye in the normal fashion and I headed off to work with no inkling of the horror the day had in store. Alan came to pick me up at the end of the day, and when we got back to the house Tom's door was shut (nothing unusual about that). But when I knocked to get his laundry, there was no reply. I tried the door and it wouldn't open, as though something heavy was in the way. I got it open a few inches and could see Tom slumped against the wall. At first I thought he'd fallen asleep, but as I shook him I realised something was seriously wrong. I shouted for Alan, who raced up the stairs and told me to call 999. He forced his way into the room. The emergency services calmly told me that we needed to do chest compressions, but Alan was already doing them and we could see it was too late; there was nothing we could do.

Nothing could have prepared us for the scene in front of us. Our beloved 16 year old son had committed suicide. It was real. It was happening to us.

The paramedics arrived; one of whom just happened to be the same one who had treated Tom just a few weeks earlier, after he'd got drunk. It felt like God's grace that there was a familiar face in such unfamiliar territory. They asked us to leave the room while they did what they needed to do, and so we sat on our bed and read the letters that Tom had left in his room for us. There were two addressed to us – it turned out he'd written one of them before his previous suicide attempt. He said we weren't to blame ourselves, but that he was unable to cope in the real world and, 'the sooner I meet God, the better.' He said he'd never feared death because he knew he'd go to heaven, and he ended the letter with, 'I'll see you later!' knowing that we would one day join him there.

We were trying to process what was going on when the phone rang. It was James, letting us know he was leaving work. We couldn't tell him over the phone what had happened. 'Come home,' we said quietly. 'Drive carefully.' There followed the phone calls no parent should have to make where we could only say, 'Tom's dead,' to our pastor, my parents and our closest friend. They dropped everything and got to the house as quickly as they could, not knowing the manner of his death.

The paramedics gave us time to say goodbye. Our family doctor happened to be on call for the police that day, and he reassured us that Tom's death was as peaceful as it could have been. There were no signs of a struggle; he had meant to be successful with this attempt. We had turned off the music that had been blaring out and I could feel that there was a deep peace in the room. The darkness had lifted. I kissed Tom's forehead in the way I'd done so many times over the years when I'd said goodnight. 'Silly boy. Silly, silly boy,' I kept whispering over and over as I touched him one last time in the most heart-breaking of moments.

Even in those overwhelming first few hours, we had a real sense of God's closeness. The fact that we knew the paramedic, the doctor and even the policeman who had been called to the scene helped enormously. We later found out that after we called Phil, our pastor, a prayer chain had been put in place and those prayers seemed to surround and uphold us in a bubble of peace. We never blamed God for what happened, not even then. We didn't blame Tom either.

Along with his letter, Tom had left us a journal (which he called his 'suicide file') detailing his private thoughts. We found it the day after his death and poured over every agonising word, suddenly seeing into the dark places of our son's mind. We read about what he called his 'unending river of pain and emotion', his depression and anger. He wrote: 'Life is about pain. You go from heartache to heartbreak, each time sinking deeper into the emptiness'. At times he railed against God, but then said things like, 'I feel God's love and no one else's and that's why I need to die. When I am dead I will be able to physically see the only one whose love I can feel.'

He wrote about a belittling voice that told him people might cry for a day if he was gone but then they'd be glad. He spoke about how he'd wanted us to think he was the best son/brother/Christian he could be, so that's why he'd put on a brave face for us, even though his heart was in turmoil because he didn't know who he was. As we read, we began to understand the pain he had been in, and wished there was some way to turn the clock back and comfort him.

We could never say that taking his life was a good decision, but we have come to understand that Tom was suffering with a severe mental illness, where thoughts of suicide plagued him and it genuinely seemed like the right option to him. He even said in his letter to us that he'd never told us any of this because he didn't want to be talked out of his plans to end his life. He didn't believe he could cope with life; he never felt normal, never felt like he fitted in.

People have asked many times why Tom ended his life, but the truth is there is no one answer to that question. Bullying may have played a part but, as his letters and journal show, that wasn't the full picture. He didn't want to grow up. By the time he died at 16, he'd been struggling with his place in the world for nine years and he couldn't take any more.

Because Tom died on a Friday night, it was only 36 hours later that we set foot in church for the Sunday service. Phil (our pastor) had asked us what we wanted to do, and we said we had to be there. Where else would we go? We were aware that the whole church family knew what had happened and that all eyes would be on us, so we said we'd sneak in at the last possible minute and leave the moment the service finished so as not to make a fuss. But when we got to the church door, we realised there was none of the usual hubbub of a Sunday morning – just a weighty silence pregnant with grief. We hesitated before forcing ourselves through the doors, where we were greeted by our grieving church family. They welcomed us in, ushered us to the seats that had been saved for us, and then Phil began the service with Psalm 23, his voice breaking with emotion.

We knew even then that we had to worship God like never before. We had to turn to Him in our grief and not away, and

He gave us strength as we did. God spoke so tenderly as we came in our grief, and He poured out His love, which we so desperately needed.

Our church family surrounded us with love too, and we feel so blessed to have them. From the very first moment they heard our terrible news they overwhelmed us with love, upheld us in prayer and have never let go. They listened and didn't judge. Deep friendships are forged when you share the hard things in life. Our church understood that pulling a random Bible verse out of context and offering it as a platitude wasn't going to soothe our souls. We needed their love and support whether it came in the form of a hug, a hand held, or a cottage pie cooked for us so we didn't have to think about making dinner. Even now, so many years later, people still remember important dates like Tom's birthday and the anniversary of his death, and they check in with us. They've let us be real and say when we've had an awful week. They've never expected us to plaster on the fake smiles we'd seen religious people do when we were growing up. They cry with us rather than assuming that we've 'got over it' and don't need to talk about Tom anymore. We can't see how we could have survived Tom's suicide if it wasn't for them.

But that's not to say it wasn't hell. It was. We're not super-spiritual people. We've struggled. This pain has taken us to the very brink of what we could cope with. We found it hard to read our Bibles. We found it hard to pray. We took comfort in remembering that even spiritual heroes like Mother Teresa sometimes felt like her prayers bounced off the ceiling. Sometimes we'd stand in church and try to worship but we could barely get the words out of our mouths. The longing of our hearts was that we would always praise God for His goodness; the reality was that sometimes we weren't sure if we even believed the words we were singing. But we kept going to church, even when our hearts felt so broken that it was the last place we wanted to be. We went out of obedience until we wanted to be there again. We chose to worship until we wanted to worship. We let the sermons float over us until we were able to engage with them again. We felt like we could bring very little on a Sunday but desperately needed to receive, and our church accepted us as we were. We tried to hold on to the fact that it was OK for us to just be how we were.

Shortly after Tom's death, Alan and I both took on new jobs at a retreat centre but it was a disaster. My self-confidence plummeted and I began to sink into a depression. By the summer, I couldn't leave the house and was overwhelmed with suicidal thoughts of my own. I made a plan. I bought pills and wine and chose the night I would do it. I told Alan I was fine and insisted he go out to a party, thinking that would be the perfect opportunity for me to take my life. I sat at the top of the stairs, ready to end things, when I suddenly felt surrounded by the most amazing love and peace. Up until then I would have said that I knew God loved me, but it was only at that lowest moment that I truly *knew* it.

When Alan came home, I told him what had happened and agreed to get help. He said, 'I've lost a son – I don't want to lose my wife as well.' Anti-depressants helped me get back on an even keel, but there was a rift in our marriage. When a couple lose a child, there's an 80% chance their marriage will break down. I didn't want to be part of that statistic, but I could see no way out. Alan and I had been really close in the immediate aftermath of Tom's death; we'd clung to each other closer than ever before. But over time, our grief began to push us apart. I didn't want to deal with what was happening in my head, and I began to understand why Tom had kept so many of his thoughts to himself. Saying them aloud would make them real so I internalised them, which unfortunately only gave them more power. I desperately wanted Alan to hold me in a huge hug, but somehow I couldn't say that – and the signals I was giving him suggested I wanted him to stay away.

It's taken a lot of time, effort and support from others, but things have turned around and now we're doing really well. We share the privilege (and pressure!) of running a tearoom together. Each table has a copy of our story alongside the menu, which opens up all sorts of conversations. Some people just come in for tea, but because we've been real about the pain in our lives, people often feel able to share their pain with us. It creates a wonderfully honest atmosphere; God does something special when we lay aside the image we think we need to project and instead let people see us as we really are.

We've seen God meet with us in beautiful ways in our pain. In the early days there were practical things, like Tom's body being released for burial far quicker than would normally happen, or the organ being broken in the crematorium meaning we could have a band (as would have been Tom's preference). Other times it's been less tangible – an awareness of people praying that has lifted us and helped us carry on, or a heartfelt hug that has ministered God's goodness and nearness to us. Sometimes it has felt like we're hanging onto God by our fingernails, but we've still hung on.

There have been times when we questioned what we could have done differently, but we know those thoughts will only torture us further; they won't bring Tom back. Allowing those thoughts free reign in your mind is like pressing a self-destruct button. You just have to accept what has happened, even though it is the most unfathomable thing in the world. This whole experience, though horrendous, has given us a deeper trust in God; the absolute worst happened and we're still here, so we know we can keep going, no matter what. We could keep protesting that it's not fair we don't have our son anymore – and of course it's not – but we have to keep going, acknowledging the pain as we do. One thing we've learned is that you never 'get over' losing someone you love. The pain is always there, but over time you adjust to a new normal – whatever 'normal' is. Some days we're OK, others we don't want to get out of bed or talk to anyone. We don't feel brave or courageous. We're just two normal people trying to keep going and deal with what has happened to our family.

We think it's important to share our story because there's so much stigma still attached to depression and suicide, and that doesn't help anyone. Some people think that because Tom was a Christian, he shouldn't have had these dark thoughts about suicide – but sadly none of us are immune. Tom loved Jesus, but he still struggled with his mental health. I knew first-hand the devastation that suicide causes, but I was still desperate enough to contemplate it myself.

We need to create safe places for people to be honest about their struggles and ongoing pain. People often worry about what they will say to someone who has suffered a tragic loss. From our experience, it's better to say something than nothing. In the days and weeks after Tom's death, we had people we'd known for years cross the road to avoid us. One friend said they didn't know what to say, but took my hand and squeezed it – and, truthfully, that ministered more to me than even the most eloquent of words could have. You don't have to find the right words because there are no right words – some pain goes beyond words – you just need to be willing to sit with people in their grief, love them as they are, and slowly journey towards healing together.

You can read more of Jackie and Alan's story in Jackie Slough, *Losing Tom, Finding Grace* (West Horsley: Onwards and Upwards Publishers Ltd, 2011).

CHAPTER 5

LETTING GO OF PAIN

When I was three years old, my little brother Matthew came into the world. My mum's body was producing antibodies to fight the pregnancy, thinking it was a risk to her, so he arrived four weeks early. The same complication had occurred when mum was pregnant with me, and though the doctors warned my parents that I might have developmental issues, after eight days in the special care baby unit, I was fine. Sadly, though, it wasn't the same for Matthew. His lungs hadn't had time to develop fully, and he died just a few days after arriving in the world – one day before my third birthday.

My parents, of course, were utterly devastated. They didn't even get to hold him. I don't have many memories of that time as I was so young, but every year after that, we would struggle to celebrate my birthday. I knew that 11 March held a sad significance for our family as we remembered Matthew, and it seemed wrong to throw ourselves into presents and parties the very next day. I spent a lot of my childhood wondering how things would have turned out had Matthew lived. I was fortunate to have a younger sister, who I loved to bits – but she wasn't football mad like I was. I always thought Matthew would have been as keen on sport as I was, and we would have spent many happy hours kicking a ball around in the garden.

The feeling of sadness about Matthew didn't leave me. I vividly remember my sixteenth birthday, when my mum and dad sorted out some food, and then left me and a big group of friends to celebrate at our house. It was meant to be a happy time, yet halfway through the evening I was overwhelmed with sadness. I couldn't hide it and I didn't know what to do – I just knew I couldn't stay. I couldn't face anyone, so I hid in my room until they all left. I had buried my pain over the years, feeling like it wasn't my place to grieve. I hadn't spoken to anyone about how I was feeling, thinking I was being selfish. Surely if anyone had a right to be in pain it was my parents; what I was dealing with was nothing in comparison. So I'd stayed quiet, wishing the sadness would just disappear.

We so often play that game when it comes to pain and grief: 'I shouldn't feel this way because someone else has had it worse.' It never works. It's like a game of Top Trumps, where you compete over who has the highest ranking to try and win your opponent's card. With grief, we'll always find someone whose pain 'trumps' ours, but belittling our own pain doesn't actually help the other person at all – all it does is force us to squash down how we're feeling. It will always resurface somewhere, somehow, and usually at a totally unexpected time.

FACING UP TO PAIN

Sadly, I didn't learn from this experience, and faced a similar problem when Diane had a miscarriage a few years ago. My gut reaction was to think, *Why should I be struggling when it's Diane who has been through the trauma?*

I will never forget the day it happened. We already had our three wonderful children – Keziah, Daniel and Abigail – but we really felt that a fourth child would complete our family, so we were delighted when Diane discovered she was pregnant. But then Diane started to bleed. She wasn't too concerned, as it was fairly light and had happened in her previous pregnancy with no further complications – but when it continued, she knew she ought to get herself checked out. I was at work when I received a text that simply said, 'Sorry, babe'. My heart sank. I instantly knew what had happened and phoned Diane straightaway, but she couldn't speak through her tears. I felt useless; totally unable to comfort her in her grief. And I felt guilty for all the times I had been worried about how we would have coped with another child, as if that could have somehow brought about the miscarriage. But most of all I felt awful for Diane; she had carried our child, and now it was gone.

As the father in this situation, I felt a real mix of emotions. My main concern was for Diane. I kept saying to myself, 'I must be the strong one', but of course I was grieving as well. Since I hadn't physically carried the child, I assumed my pain must be nothing compared to Diane's, so I tried to bury it as much as possible. I also wanted to put on a brave face for our three other children as I was worried how they would react, and I wanted to be strong for them in the face of such sad news. To make matters worse, this was all during the time my dad was in hospital with cancer (having undergone four operations in nine weeks), and he was extremely weak. I didn't want to tell him or the rest of the family about the miscarriage, as I knew how upset they would be. The baby had been a light on the horizon during a dark time for us. All of my concerns were focused on how everyone else was feeling as I continued to try to ignore my own grief.

Diane had to return to the hospital for a further procedure. She didn't want me to go with her; she just wanted to be on her own. When I picked her up afterwards, all she was able to say was that it had gone smoothly. I desperately wanted to talk, but at the same time I wanted to support her and respect her wishes. She later told me that she had been put on the same ward as those having a planned termination, and had frequently been referred to as someone who was 'terminating her pregnancy'. It made it sound like a choice she was making – and that couldn't have been further from the truth. We decided to give the baby a name. We both had a strong feeling the baby was a boy, and so we called him Joel.

I didn't know what to do with the feelings I had around the miscarriage. It didn't help when I tried to talk about it. One friend said to me, 'It's just one of those things; it's a lot worse for the woman.' My primary emotion was anger, largely directed at God, wondering how He could allow this to happen. Anger is a natural response to pain, but we're rarely taught how to manage that anger and express it in a healthy way. I thought the good Christian thing to do was to push those feelings aside, but unfortunately they refused to go away.

I would imagine picking up objects and hurling them at the wall, but then I would immediately feel guilty. Suppressing my emotions didn't seem to be working.

You might remember the TV series *Only Fools and Horses*, one of the most beloved British comedies of all time. There's a very moving scene in the 1996 Christmas Special, after Rodney and Cassandra have suffered a miscarriage. Rodney is unable to talk about it, thinking the best solution is to bury his emotions deep down. When Del finally gets him to open up, Rodney says: 'We were looking forward and all we could see in front of us was a big wide highway and we were just cruising like we were in a Rolls-Royce. And suddenly it came to a shattering halt… I've never felt s*dding pain like that in all my life.' He goes on to say, 'It's almost like if I don't talk about it, it might not be true.'[1]

While miscarriage happens frequently (current estimates say that around one in four recognised pregnancies miscarry, with 85% of those happening in the first 12 weeks[2]) there aren't that many people speaking openly about it, particularly from the point of view of the father. That's a lot of pain and sadness that isn't being addressed. I wanted to share something of our experience to stand with those who have known this type of loss. Everyone reacts differently, but it can be a great source of strength to know you are not alone, and that others understand what you're going through. We need to keep reminding one another that it's actually healthy to express our pain, anger and fear, and that God is with us and loves us, no matter what is going on.

Sometimes we'd rather numb our pain than look at it or try

to deal with it. We'd rather forget by watching hours of Netflix; take the edge off with a shopping trip or a few glasses of wine. But pain that isn't dealt with doesn't disappear, and we can't ignore it forever. Pain can rob us of the deep joy that God has for us. Brené Brown explains it like this:

'Pain will subside only when we acknowledge it and care for it. Addressing it with love and compassion would take only a minuscule percentage of the energy it takes to fight it, but approaching pain head-on is terrifying... Most of us were not taught how to recognise pain, name it and be with it... we were taught anger, rage, and denial instead. But... when we deny our emotion, it owns us. When we own our emotion, we can rebuild and find our way through the pain.'[3]

THE CLIMB

I've already mentioned how, for me, anxiety manifests itself as a feeling of falling into a bottomless pit, or of trying to climb out of a huge hole. Sometimes I've been aware that my struggle to get out of that hole is exacerbated by the extra baggage I'm carrying, which weighs me down. Climbing out while it's still on my back feels impossible.

My sadness regarding Matthew stayed with me like an extra weight on my back into my adulthood and it always made Diane upset that it marred my birthday celebrations, even though she understood why it impacted me. I had people pray for me about it, yet this deep sadness remained. It was at one of my counselling sessions that the subject came up again, and my psychologist suggested that writing a letter to Matthew might help. My immediate reaction was, *What a stupid idea.*

As you may have gathered, talking and writing about my feelings doesn't come easily to me. I'm perfectly familiar with the theory that 'talking is good', but doing it is another matter altogether! Part of me thought I was being too soft about Matthew and needed to toughen up and get over it. But I had to admit that trying to tough it out hadn't got me very far – positive talk wasn't shifting the emptiness – so I bit the bullet and tried my psychologist's suggestion. I put pen to paper and started to write to Matthew about how much I missed him, how I wished he was around to meet Diane and our kids, and how I felt he had been stolen from me. I acknowledged that it felt like my life had been designed to have him in it and maybe, if he was around, I would be a better person. When Matthew died, some people unhelpfully told my dad, 'God must have wanted him to take him so soon.' My dad's reply was, 'I wanted him as well.' I echoed that sentiment even all those years later.

I took the letter to the cemetery and buried it, praying, 'God I don't understand why You would create someone just to take them again. If it was the devil, why didn't you stop him? But I release Matthew to You now.' I got a couple of very strange looks from others in the graveyard, but to my own astonishment I left feeling differently. Things slowly started to change, and I started to enjoy my birthdays a lot more. It wasn't as though all the pain disappeared overnight, but that letter and prayer was part of a slow process of allowing God to heal me. Sometimes we think we want God to hit us over the head with healing, but He is far gentler, not wanting to control us but to gently lead us to a quiet place where we can hear His voice whispering His gentle care to us.

Best-selling novel *The Shack* describes pain in a way that rings so true to me: 'Pain has a way of clipping our wings and keeping us from being able to fly, and left unresolved for very long, you can almost forget that you were created to fly in the first place.'[4] I can see those clipped wings in my own life but also in the lives of many of the young people and families I have worked with over the years. They can't seem to get free; they can't seem to enter into something new because they can't let go of past brokenness.

JUST IMAGINE...

Some Christian counsellors help people to release past pain by using imagery work. This is usually most effective in an environment where the person being counselled feels safe and comfortable, as it can stir up some strong emotions. With your eyes closed, you let your mind revisit a memory that might have triggered some of the pain you are currently feeling. When my psychologist suggested we try this, I was thinking, *Oh, please God, no.* I don't have much of an imagination and I didn't expect to see anything but, to my complete surprise, I had a crystal-clear image and the pain that came with it from remembering that time brought me to tears.

What came to mind was a school PE lesson, which took place when I was about 11. My PE teacher liked to shout a lot, and this particular time, I was the one in the firing line of his anger. We were learning the discus, and I really struggled to get the hang of what I was doing; I just couldn't get the knack of how to hold it, or release it. The teacher was getting more and more frustrated with me, until he just lost it and started yelling at me as loudly as he could in front of the whole class. I wasn't particularly academic at school, so I took a lot of pride in being good at PE – I was the school sports captain. As I stood there in front of the class, being shouted at for something I couldn't control, I felt utterly humiliated. Tears were stinging my eyes and, to my horror, I couldn't stop them from coming out. My humiliation was complete as I began to cry in front of the class. Even then, my teacher carried on shouting. I have never felt so embarrassed and ashamed.

My psychologist asked me to try and imagine how Jesus would respond if He came into that scene. What would He say? What would I tell Him? How would it make me feel to have Him there? (If you find it hard to picture Jesus, psychologists suggest thinking of your older self or a person you love, like a close friend, instead.) I 'looked', and I could see someone going up to the teacher and saying in a firm voice, 'That's *my* boy,' while pointing to me. It was surreal to see Him defending me, saying, 'You can't talk to my boy like that; he is special to me.' It feels odd to write about it now, but it made such a huge difference to me to know that while God isn't all that interested in how far I can throw a discus, He is fully invested in me and my feelings.

Memories can often stop us doing things that we would love to do because we fear that history will repeat itself.

When we are young, our brains are like sponges, absorbing all kinds of experiences – and we often come to the wrong conclusions about ourselves and others because of things spoken to us or over us, and things that happen. Anxiety is sometimes the result of unresolved pain from the past, and misunderstandings about who we are and our place in the world. It can be a symptom of something else going on underneath the surface.

Without forcing anything, allow God to bring to mind a time when you may have needed more love and support than you were given, and allow Him into that memory in order to bring healing. Whatever you've been through you can bring to Him, and ask Him to speak to you about how He would have responded if you had seen Him there in that situation. You belong to Him, and He loves you. Let Him bring that love and healing to your past pains.

DEALING WITH ANGER

One of the problems with unacknowledged pain is that it often causes anger, and if we see anger as a sin (as I used to), we will find it difficult to bring it to God. In order to be able to express our anger in a healthy way, we have to realise that God can handle it. It's not sinful to feel anger, but if we don't deal with it in the right way, it can lead to sinful behaviour. As Christians, we need to talk about anger; it's something many of us struggle with.

I received this email from a couple who were trying to process some deep pain and anger:

My husband Wayne and I were trying for a baby for a long time. My sister had a clear prophetic word that we would fall pregnant on 22 February 2016. Two weeks after that date, we did a pregnancy test. We were so used to them reading negative that when this one was positive I used every spare stick I could find just to be sure! We were so excited and thankful. God was great.

However, one day at work, I started bleeding. We went to hospital for a scan, and they told us the hardest words to hear: there was no heartbeat. I would not let them operate, hoping they had made a mistake or that God was going to breathe life back into our baby. However, it was not to be.

We were angry at God. We still believed in God, but thought He was cruel. I thought He must have been punishing me. My husband thought God was a God of hate, not love, and said he might as well go back to living like he used to. (Before he was a Christian, Wayne was violent and a thief; he didn't understand why God had turned His back on him when he had turned his life around.) We didn't know why God had promised us a baby, then taken it away. Not very helpfully, we were told we should have prayed more. We had prayed every day for that baby. We hated God but couldn't tell anyone how we really felt.

Then, by 'chance', we came across an advert for your DVD. Wayne ordered it and said it was worth a go, but it was the only chance God was getting. It arrived and we watched it in silence, in tears. It told us it was OK to be angry at God; we weren't the only ones. He wasn't cruel and He wasn't angry at us for being angry with Him. Then God spoke to Wayne. He said our baby was a girl, and that He'd given us the date

> not to be cruel but so that we knew she counted as a life. He said it makes no difference to Him whether the baby was just conceived or died at 100; a life is a life. He said if He gave us the date of the baby we would hold in the future, then we would not have known if our little girl counted. God reassured us that she was in heaven and we would see her when we got there. He also said that by 2017 we would have another baby.
>
> I doubted Him as our first one took so long, but as I am writing this, I am due next month. The whole experience has changed our view of God, and dying. I used to be scared of me or my husband dying, but now we joke that the first one to heaven gets to hold our little girl first.
>
> Thank you again for such an honest and real DVD.
>
> Rachel

Many people like Rachel and Wayne don't feel that there is a place for them, as Christians, to express their anger with God. Though anger isn't talked about much in church, the Bible doesn't shy away from the topic. The apostle Paul says: '"In your anger do not sin": do not let the sun go down while you are still angry, and do not give the devil a foothold' (Eph. 4:26–27). In other words, anger in itself isn't a sin, but hanging on to it is. Solomon said, 'anger *resides* in the lap of fools' (Eccl. 7:9, emphasis added); the word 'resides' implying that we shouldn't let anger become a resident when it should only ever be a visitor.

We need to grasp that getting angry with God, and acknowledging the thoughts that are tearing us apart, is OK. God is big enough to deal with it. Getting angry means we stay engaged with God and we find release; pretending we're OK can drive a huge wedge into our relationship with Him. If we let it, anger can drive us into God's presence in our search for answers, and there we find there is no need for pretence; we are free to express everything we're feeling before a God who knows and loves us.

TRUSTING IN GOD'S TIMING

In chapter 3, I briefly touched on the extraordinary life of Joseph, and how he spent so many years waiting, not really knowing what the future would look like. As I reflect on that story, I wonder how Joseph felt about his brothers, and the deep pain he must have felt at their betrayal. If he'd wanted to find them, then by the time he was second command in Egypt, he would certainly have had the resources – so I wonder if he regretted his own actions and the way he had behaved with them, too. Living with regrets is incredibly painful. Hurting someone in a way that I can't seem to fix is, for me, one of the hardest things to deal with. Maybe Joseph wanted to see reconciliation, or maybe he was still hurting and knew it had to be in God's timing; either way, his family was completely broken.

Pharaoh's dream predicted seven years of famine, and it was due to this famine that Joseph's older brothers had to travel all the way to Egypt to buy grain. Twenty years had passed since their betrayal, so they didn't recognise Joseph, who would have been wearing the clothes of Egyptian royalty. Imagine the emotions Joseph felt as the brothers who sold him into slavery all those years ago finally stood in front of him.

Before Joseph revealed who he was, he tested them – perhaps to see if they had changed, or showed remorse for what they had done to him. He made it look as though their youngest brother, Benjamin, had stolen a special cup – and told them to go back home to Canaan without him. Joseph was giving them the opportunity to do to Benjamin what they had done to him: abandon him. But this time Judah stepped forward, offering to give his life as a slave if Benjamin could be set free (Gen. 44:34).

At this point, Joseph could no longer control himself; he made everyone else leave him, and then came the moment he made himself known to his brothers. He hadn't stored up bitterness to be unleashed in a torrent of anger over the way they treated him. He held all the power, but instead of punishing them, he offered the hand of forgiveness and reconciliation. He wept loudly as he told them, 'do not be distressed and do not be angry with yourselves for selling me here, because it was to save lives that God sent me ahead of you' (Gen. 45:5).

Joseph continued to trust God throughout his life, despite all the evidence that may have suggested God had abandoned him. Tim Keller says this:

> *'Standing where we do, we can look back and ask whether God was really "missing in action" all of those years when he seemed to be absent from Joseph's life. When Joseph prayed for his life in that cistern, did God really not hear him? And all those years when absolutely everything*

seemed to go wrong for Joseph, was God not there? No, he was there, and he was working. He was hidden, but he was also in complete control.'[5]

Trusting in God's timing is tough. And while it's easy enough to write that we should trust God with our pain, it's something that can actually take many years to work through. The encouragement is we don't go through it alone. God takes us on a journey. He doesn't expect us to go from 0 to 60 in two seconds and immediately reach perfection, as we so often expect ourselves to. So let's keep reminding each another that it's actually healthy to express our pain, anger and fear, and that God is with us and loves us no matter what's going on.

Wayne and Rachel had a healthy baby boy. They called him Noah Samuel, which means 'rest and comfort in hearing God', and 'being heard by God'.

CHAPTER 6

LETTING GO OF PERFECTION

After I'd been seeing my psychologist for a while, she noticed a trend in the way I spoke to and about myself. I was rarely kind. 'You are putting yourself under huge amounts of pressure,' she said. 'You need to show yourself some self-compassion.'

She wasn't the first to say it. My mentor used to say to me, 'You need to put your own oxygen mask on first,' but that never sat very easily with me. It seemed more appropriate to help others and not worry about yourself. But Diane would regularly tell me that I needed to be kinder to myself, so after my psychologist said it too, I thought I would try to keep them happy by making a list of things I liked doing. It wasn't exactly a long list, but I wrote that I liked watching football, walking the dog, and going to the cinema. I hoped that if I did these things occasionally, it would be enough to get everyone off my back and stop them talking about all this self-compassion stuff.

When I spoke to my psychologist, she gently pointed out that I had completely misunderstood what self-compassion is really all about. When I researched it more thoroughly, I realised that true self-compassion goes a whole lot deeper than simply doing the odd thing we enjoy. The first thing I discovered is what self-compassionate is *not*. Self-compassion is not the same thing as self-indulgence, which focuses on giving yourself endless pleasure. When we say 'be kind to yourself', we often mean 'have that extra glass of wine if you're having a bad day', or 'don't worry if you've eaten a whole packet of biscuits, you deserved it'. This kind of thing may not be a big deal if only done occasionally, but real self-compassion is about wanting ourselves to flourish in the long term. Many of our ways of showing 'kindness' to ourselves actually damage us in the long run, not to mention that short-term pleasure is often quickly followed by feelings of guilt, which make us feel even worse.

We also have to be careful that we don't mistake self-pity for self-compassion. When we give in to self-pity, everything becomes about us – what we feel, what we want, why no one else understands us, and why our suffering is worse than anyone else's. Self-pity is inward-looking in an unhealthy way, and causes us to lose perspective and potentially make a drama out of everything so that we can be the star of the show.

Self-esteem and self-compassion are also different. Self-esteem is about our sense of worth and our understanding of our value. For many of us, our self-esteem fluctuates according to what the world thinks of us; we feel judged on how we look, how impressive our career is, how many Instagram followers we have, or what we can afford to buy. Self-compassion, however, is not about outside influences – it is something you can always exercise towards yourself. It's about recognising that you are a flawed human being, and that you are suffering – and, rather than beating yourself up, extending kindness to yourself. Most people find it easy to be compassionate towards others. If someone else is suffering, we're quick to try to help make things better. If they are ill, we encourage them to rest and sleep. If they are feeling bad about themselves, we try to silence their inner critic by reminding them of their gifts and strengths, encouraging them not to set unrealistic expectations of what they can achieve. Compassion means to 'suffer with'. We comfort and care when we see need in others, but do we do the same for ourselves? How often do we pile on the pain by criticising ourselves and the way we're handling a situation? Are we quick to forgive ourselves for mistakes, or do we pick over them for hours, finding a catalogue of faults we can berate ourselves for? Do we acknowledge we're in pain and that it's OK not to be OK, or do we constantly tell ourselves to get over it already?

Kristin Neff gave a fantastic TEDx talk, which she titled 'The Space Between Self-Esteem and Self-Compassion'. In her talk she explains that when we're struggling, we need to treat ourselves as we would treat a good friend – with encouragement, understanding, empathy, patience and gentleness. But instead, we so often say things to ourselves that we wouldn't ever say to someone we don't like very much – let alone someone we love. She says:

> 'Instead of mercilessly judging and criticizing yourself for various inadequacies or shortcomings, self-compassion means you're kind and understanding when confronted with personal failings – after all, who ever said you were supposed to be perfect?'[1]

'NOT ENOUGH'

I am much more likely to think about my failures than my successes; I spend far too much time thinking about what I've done wrong, and going over situations I think I should have handled better. I worry about people I may have upset, and all the ways I'm not up to the job.

Having led XLP since the very beginning, I never felt like a 'proper' CEO – I never had an interview, and I never had to prove to someone I could do the job before they gave it to me. I've always believed that any success XLP has had has been down to the rest of the team. After one talk I gave, someone gave us £30k – but it didn't feel right to take any credit. I've been on the radio a number of times when similar things have happened afterwards, but no amount of affirmation ever really helps. I have what is known as 'imposter syndrome'; you feel that everything good you have done is just a fluke, and one day you will be found out for being the fraud and failure that you are (or so you believe).

One thing that has always made me feel hugely insecure is that I am not very academic. A few years ago, I invited a speaker from the US (who I really admired) to come and talk to our team. I was so excited about his visit that I insisted all of our staff be there, and invited some friends of ours to join us too. I had read all of this guy's books and couldn't wait for what he would bring to us.

When the speaker began to address us, he said, 'I'm going to go around the room and I want each of you to tell me what your degree is in.' My heart sank. I just wanted to get out of there, but there was no hiding. I sat and listened as my amazing team all spoke about their qualifications while he wrote them down on his clipboard. Then he smiled at me.

'Patrick, tell everyone what degree you have.'

I kept my head low and almost silently muttered, 'I don't have a degree.'

Thankfully, my marketing manager faked shock and jokingly shouted, 'What?!' as loudly as he could, and everyone laughed. The moment passed and we moved on, but still I felt like my personal shame had been hung out for everyone to see.

I would frequently go home from XLP believing I was not enough. I would constantly criticise myself for not being intelligent enough to understand everything that was happening in every meeting. I questioned whether I was really the right person to make decisions about things like HR or child protection. I once got asked to write a policy paper as part of a group, and so I was in and out of Westminster, working with serious academics. I would sit in the House of Commons thinking, *What on earth am I doing here?* That voice in your head can be so damaging. Diane used to say to me, 'Would you treat one of your gap-year students or one of the young people you work with the way you treat yourself?' I knew I wouldn't – in fact, I would be furious if I heard anyone speak to them the way I speak to myself! – but I was setting myself unrelenting standards that I couldn't ever live up to. I struggled to show myself any self-compassion, refused to validate my feelings, and didn't stand up to others when they tapped (sometimes unknowingly) into my self-condemnation.

When you're stuck in this mindset and your sensitivity is on high alert, you can perceive things to be criticism even when they aren't meant to be. The feeling of not being enough plays on a constant loop. When we constantly attack ourselves, something damaging occurs to us physically as well as mentally. The human brain often interprets criticism as threat, and in response it produces a chemical called cortisol for a 'fight or flight' reaction. When we are the ones criticising ourselves, we are in the position of being both the attacker and the attacked – so we're producing an even higher amount of cortisol. If you are in this mode regularly, you'll have high levels of stress, which can cause the body to shut itself down by becoming depressed in order to protect itself.

Self-compassion, however, seems to be one of the major keys to recovering from pain and trauma. Author Sheryl Sandberg says:

> 'Those who can tap into it [self-compassion] recover from hardship faster. In a study of people whose marriages fell apart, resilience was not related to their self-esteem, optimism, or depression before divorce, or to how long their relationships or separations had lasted. What helped people cope with distress and move on was self-compassion. For soldiers returning from war in Afghanistan and Iraq, those who were kind to themselves showed significant declines in symptoms of post-traumatic stress disorder (PTSD). Self-compassion is associated with greater happiness and satisfaction, fewer emotional difficulties, and less anxiety.'[2]

'IT HAS TO BE PERFECT'

If you like things to be perfect, here's some bad news: you can't be self-compassionate and be a perfectionist. The two just aren't compatible. Anne Wilson Schaef says, 'Perfectionism is self-abuse of the highest order.'[3]

Perfectionism makes everything catastrophic. The smallest thing – such as a disagreement with a friend or a minimal mistake at work – becomes the end of the world. Perfectionists set up unrealistic expectations for themselves, and striving to meet those targets becomes addictive and all-consuming. Then what we find is that the goalposts are constantly moving anyway. I'm always striving to get one area of my life sorted, thinking that once I do I'll be content – only to find that I'm then consumed with sorting the next thing, and so on. I'm trying to learn that it's OK to be imperfect, that I'm allowed to make mistakes, and that regardless of how much I mess up, I am loved unconditionally. When we let go of the unrealistic image of who we think we're supposed to be, we can get on with being the unique person God created us to be. In his book on perfectionism, my friend Will van der Hart says this:

> 'Perfectionism thrives when you believe that you are more in control than you really are, which is also, ironically, the illusion that perfectionism wants to offer you. Many Christians struggling with perfectionism fear that they are "letting themselves off the hook" or "passing the buck" if they assume less than complete responsibility for everything.'[4]

There have been occasions in the last few years when I could be doing as many as 20 radio interviews in one weekend. Afterwards I would find I couldn't sleep because I was going over and over again in my head how I could have answered the questions better. After much tossing and turning, Diane would ask me why I couldn't sleep, and I'd answer that I was worried I'd messed up the radio interview. 'You probably didn't,' she'd tell me, 'but even if you didn't answer it perfectly, it doesn't matter. You did the best you can, you always do the best you can, and you don't have to be perfect. Instead of thinking about what you might or might not have done wrong, why not think about the fact that you put yourself out there in front of hundreds of thousands of people to talk on behalf of the young people you work with. I am proud of you, and I believe God is proud of you too.'

As lovely and important as it is to hear kind words from other people, we need to be the ones who ultimately let ourselves off the hook – that's what self-compassion is all about. We need to tell the loud inner critic to be quiet, and listen to the quieter voice of compassion. The next time you feel you've messed up, remind yourself that no one is perfect. The only thing we can do is our best, and making a mistake doesn't make us a complete failure – it makes us human. When we're having a down day, rather than telling ourselves to cheer up, let's acknowledge some of the things that are making life hard, and remind ourselves that it's perfectly normal to feel sad, angry, despondent or confused. Let's give ourselves a break from the constant high standards. We don't have to be available to others 24/7. We don't have to feel bad for not looking at our work emails during our evenings and weekends. We don't have to say yes to absolutely everything we're asked to do. Sometimes we need to put self-care higher up the agenda, knowing that it's good sense, not selfishness, which encourages us to look after ourselves.

A good friend once sent me a message on a day when I really needed to hear it. It said this:

'Note to self. The plan is this: you do what you can, when you can, however you can, with whatever you've got. And if you can't, you can't. You rest until you can again. You give yourself kindness so your pockets are full and you can reach in and pull out a fistful to offer the folks you meet along the way.'

Self-compassion isn't taking the easy way out, it's giving ourselves the kindness we need so that we're able to be kind to others.

GOD USES THE IMPERFECT

God never expects us to be perfect, and the Bible shows us His way of often choosing those who are less than perfect to work with Him. Among His chosen men and women in the Bible were people who had serious character flaws, questionable relationships, crippling insecurities, doubt, disobedience, mixed motivations and personal ambition.

One of my favourite stories is that of Gideon in Judges 6. The Israelites had let God down again, so He gave them into the hands of Midianites and they spent much of their time hiding in caves. They had to abandon their homes as everywhere they went they got invaded, their land was in ruin, and their livestock was killed. Imagine how abandoned the Israelites must have felt; how high their anxiety was, wondering when the next attack was coming; how overwhelmed they must have been after so much had gone wrong all at once. Not only that, they were hungry and couldn't seem to grow anything.

The people cried out to God (v7) and He sent a prophet to remind them of His faithfulness, and that they were part of a huge story where God was moving. Then came this interesting conversation between Gideon and the angel of the Lord:

> 'The angel of the LORD came and sat down under the oak in Ophrah that belonged to Joash the Abiezrite, where his son Gideon was threshing wheat in a winepress to keep it from the Midianites. When the angel of the LORD appeared to Gideon, he said, "The LORD is with you, mighty warrior."
>
> "Pardon me, my lord," Gideon replied, "but if the LORD is with us, why has all this happened to us? Where are all his wonders that our ancestors told us about when they said, 'Did not the LORD bring us up out of Egypt?' But now the LORD has abandoned us and given us into the hand of Midian." The LORD turned to him and said, "Go in the strength you have and save Israel out of Midian's hand. Am I not sending you?"' **(Judg. 6:11–14)**

Just in case you missed it, Gideon wasn't beaten up for expressing his doubts and asking his questions. It was OK for him to ask why, just like so many other heroes of the faith did. Surely Abraham climbed the hill with Isaac thinking, *God, why would you give me a son only to take him away from me?* Job questioned why he had even been born if he was to face so much suffering (Job 3:16). At the burning bush, Moses asked, 'Who am I that I should go?' (Exod. 3:11) in response to his commission to free the Israelites. Mary asked how she could be pregnant when she was a virgin (Luke 1:34). All these people had moments of confusion as to what God was doing, yet somehow they chose to trust Him. They weren't perfect, but they took God at His word and were obedient to Him, even when the circumstances of their lives didn't make sense.

I love God's response to Gideon's questioning: 'Go in the strength that you have'. In other words, 'You are not perfect, you are not the finished article, but that's OK. Go as you are, weak as you feel; it will be enough because I am with you.' That's why God uses people like Gideon and people like you and me – imperfect people who know they don't have a hope of doing very much in their own strength, but who know they can depend on their perfect God. The promise God gave Gideon is the same promise He gives to His people throughout the Bible: 'I will be with you.'

I love this quote by American pastor Charles Stanley:

'God is looking for imperfect men and women who have learned to walk in moment by moment dependence on the Holy Spirit, Christians who have come to terms with their inadequacies, fears and failures.'[5]

If God is not asking us for perfection, how can we ask that of ourselves? God longs for us to be free of the voice that constantly tells us we're not good enough. He longs for us to see ourselves as He sees us. He's not blind to our imperfections but He loves us regardless. If we're good enough for Him as we are, who are we to set a different standard?

RACHEL'S STORY

I first met Rachel at the end of a When Faith Gets Shaken evening in Rayleigh, Essex. Rachel spent some time chatting to my wife, Diane, who subsequently got hold of Rachel's book, called *The Skies I'm Under*.[1] Diane said it was beautiful, and I was inspired by Rachel's honesty and how she continues to hold onto God in times of real brokenness. We invited Rachel and her husband Tim round for dinner, and discovered how their passion for life and for their family is contagious. They are another example of a couple who, despite all of life's challenges, simply want to love and be loved in a way that makes others want to do the same.

> I woke with a jolt to find a stone of uncertainty laying heavy in my heart. It was the night before my due date but I became aware that I couldn't feel my baby move. Unable to settle, I slunk out of bed so as not to disturb my husband Tim, and sat in the newly decorated nursery. The faint orange streetlight illuminated the box room as I sat in silence, surrounded by the aroma of freshly painted walls.
>
> The cot opposite was ready and waiting, with a new mobile dangling pale-coloured jungle creatures overhead. My hospital bag lay packed on the freshly laid laminate flooring, while a pine chest of drawers sat filled with sleep suits and socks that looked impossibly small.

Having spent some time working as a nurse in Uganda, my mind started reeling with the memories of problematic (even traumatic) pregnancies and births that I had witnessed. As I held my still belly, I gazed at the shadows etched by our baby's mobile on the yellow wall behind the cot. Tears began to fall as I remembered my friend Nneka playing the song *Kiss the Son* by Kevin Prosch on repeat in the aftermath of her young sister's death. Within the vacuum of the night, the song reverberated in my head. Like a mantra, I replayed the refrain: 'Though you slay me I will trust You, Lord.'

I choked out the words as tears tripped my lips and an internal battle raged. Was something wrong with my baby? Was I being irrational?

Eventually I concluded my fear was overshadowing the facts, as I had felt my baby move throughout the previous day. So I gathered my emotions and returned to bed, hoping I'd feel movement in the morning. During a sleepy conversation, Tim and I agreed that I would contact the maternity unit first thing, if nothing had changed. I lay still and enjoyed Tim's arm resting on me. Having met at a Christian youth camp, we had already enjoyed a decade together. Even our chosen careers as a doctor and a nurse seemed to complement each other. Once I had packed away my concerns in a box labelled 'it's always worse in the middle of the night', my fears subsided and I soon drifted back to sleep.

The next morning, I woke and showered – but still felt no movements. Having called the midwife, I headed to the hospital to be assessed. Soon I was on the maternity ward, perched on top of starched white sheets with a foetal monitor strapped to my stomach. Immediately hearing and seeing my baby's heartbeat pacified me. I sighed with relief and my own heart rate slowed. Tim rushed up from the elderly care ward where he was working and, on hearing the heartbeat, hurried back, suitably reassured. The midwives wanted to keep monitoring things so I was left connected, and given a small red button to press if I felt the baby kick.

I lay back and tried to rest. My head hit the cold metal bar of the NHS bed frame as I closed my eyes and remembered how I got to that point. Eight months earlier, I had popped into the supermarket on the way home from work and bought a pregnancy test. Having played my part, I left it in the bathroom of our hospital accommodation for Tim to read. He came into the living room and I saw the smile on his face immediately – we were going to have a baby!

Although I had a healthy pregnancy, I was disappointed that I didn't seem to evolve into an 'earth mother'. It felt as though I had an alien squirming in my stomach, rather than finally fulfilling my cosmic role as a woman. The whole thing felt weird, with nausea and vomiting being the cherry on the pregnancy cake.

I had finished work at 38 weeks, expectant that I would experience the nesting instinct that everyone promised. However, no scrubbing or motherly homemaking occurred. It seemed my time as a domestic goddess was firmly buried with my earlier attempts to impress my new husband.

When the midwife woke me from my daydreaming, I confessed I hadn't felt my baby move. After a short consultation, the doctor made it clear that she wanted to deliver me straightaway. I called Tim, and after a short delay, we were shown to a room on the labour ward. There I clambered into a clinical gown and my waters were broken. The doctor reassured us that all the signs indicated our baby was fine but, given I was a first-time mum, it would be safest to have an immediate caesarean.

In the minutes that followed, everyone was calm and jovial and things happened very quickly. An anaesthetist arrived and poked around my spine to insert a very big needle. Before long my legs were lifted onto the trolley fizzing and tingling, as if they no longer belonged to me. In theatre, Tim sat by my head as we chatted and joked about nothing in particular. He averted his eyes from what was happening behind the curtain erected to separate us from the lower part of my body. (Apparently, cutting people open is fine until it's your wife – then it becomes distinctly less acceptable.) The hustle and bustle of theatre continued around us. The chatter of the obstetrician and midwives was accompanied by the clatter of instruments and trolleys. The operation began and I was cut open.

Just after 2pm on Wednesday 12 October 2005, a slimy, limp baby was removed from my womb with the exclamation from the delivering doctor that we had a boy! However, our smiles soon faded when moments later I realised I couldn't hear our son cry and sent Tim to investigate. After a few moments, he took long slow steps back across the suddenly sombre theatre and lowered his head next to mine. He gently informed me that our son wasn't breathing and was being resuscitated by medical staff. The theatre was a hive of activity as I lay motionless and fearful. Minutes later I was instructed to kiss the top of my son's head before he was whisked off to the neonatal intensive care unit to be ventilated.

Then the sobbing really began. The flood of my tears hit like a tsunami and in an instant the landscape of my world became unrecognisable.

An hour later, my bed was wheeled into the neonatal intensive care unit where Tim and I watched as tubes and machines were attached to every part of our son, keeping him alive. He needed a name, so the incubator was hastily labelled 'Samuel David Wright'. For three days we watched as Sammy lingered on the brink of life and death. We stood beside his clear plastic box with our minister and my parents, praying for a miracle.

Incredibly, within a few days, Sam started making massive improvements. He no longer needed help breathing and was transferred from intensive care to the normal special care baby unit. Our little family now occupied a side room, and we could easily pick Sam up, hold him, talk to him and express our love. We bought our first digital camera and recorded every grimace, cry and expression with the joyful obsession of new parents.

When I was well enough to be discharged, I had to face going home without my son. I couldn't bear being even a short car journey away from Sam. What if he started deteriorating and we couldn't get back in time? How could I be his mum with so much distance between us? With a heavy heart and empty hands, I failed to hold back my tears during the short journey home. Stepping into our house, I shuddered. What had been a place of safety and solace a few days earlier, now felt vacant and cold. I recalled the last time I had slept in my own bed. What had happened to my little boy as he lay inside me? What could I have done differently? Tim held me as I cried, and for the following week, we felt suspended in time, unable to see a future or understand the past. We travelled between our two worlds of home and hospital, our hearts split by a short five-minute drive.

At 12 days old, the medical staff were surprised and delighted that Sam could be discharged on no medication. We felt as though we were bringing our miracle baby home. We had an MRI scan booked for Sam in ten weeks' time, but quietly we hoped everything would be fine.

A few days before Christmas, we found ourselves being led down a dark hospital corridor and into a small windowless office for the results. We were clinging onto our hopes of a miracle, praying the news from the MRI would be good. Instead it was our worst nightmare. The doctor explained that Sam had been very unlucky and that something had happened (they couldn't pinpoint what) that had severely affected his brain. I sat rigid and gazed across at the scan. I could see a withered, shrunken brain, with deep darkened rims of space where healthy tissue should have been. The doctor's words became a blur of white noise as my mind drowned out the truth, trying to identify how I had allowed this catastrophic event to occur.

It was as if the doctor had produced a paintbrush of brilliant white paint and covered the walls of our future. The vivid colours of our hopes and dreams had been abruptly erased, and the blank canvas that remained felt daunting rather than full of potential. Nothing could be assumed, and nothing could be expected. It was as though a bomb had exploded in the middle of our lives, splintering our world into a thousand tiny pieces. Like the walking wounded, we staggered out of the hospital holding onto each other, dazed and bewildered. The words spoken over us rang in our ears. I simply hadn't prepared myself for hearing that Sam had profound brain damage.

Few words fell during our tube ride home, but Tim kept a hand on me the whole way. I began to realise the extent of the assumptions I had made while carrying Sam. So many dreams and plans had sprouted as he grew in my womb. Later, as Tim and I huddled close together and talked quietly, we started to unpack the implications of the truth. We noticed that rather than the uncertainty of whether our son might go to university, we were left wondering if he would ever communicate, see, sit, walk, or eat. In a single breath, our expectations had vanished. I had to identify and lay down all my previous assumptions and start with a clean sheet. I could remain hopeful and work towards the unexpected, but in order to manage my feelings I decided to anticipate nothing. I knew it would be harder and more draining to be repeatedly disappointed, to compare life with what I felt it should have been. All of the 'first' milestones a parent would normally look forward to, take photos of and post on Facebook, had been taken from us. I had left them in a small office in the depths of Hammersmith Hospital, along with many dreams. I was going to have to work out a new selection of 'firsts' that I could celebrate, unique to the world I would occupy with my family.

For us it was disability; for some it is dementia, the loss of a loved one or career opportunity. Most people, at some point, hear news that unexpectedly changes their life for the worse. It is that moment when the cart you are sitting in launches down the rollercoaster on an unexpected and stomach-churning ride.

The holocaust survivor and psychiatrist Viktor Frankl said this:

'We must never forget that we may also find meaning in life even when confronted with a hopeless situation, when facing a fate that cannot be changed. For what then matters is to bear witness to the uniquely human potential at its best, which is to transform a personal tragedy into a triumph, to turn one's predicament into a human achievement. When we are no longer able to change a situation—just think of an incurable disease such as inoperable cancer—we are challenged to change ourselves.' [2]

I had a lot of changing to do: I had to learn to live in a new kind of normal. A couple of weeks after Sam's MRI scan, I was standing by the kitchen sink chatting with a friend. Partway through our conversation, I put down my soap-covered crockery and looked her in the eye: 'I'm never going to write a book.' It may have been an odd claim, but I wanted to underline how adamant I was that if God thought He was doing this so that I could one day help others, He had another think coming. Fast-forward ten years and my memoir, *The Skies I'm Under*, was published. It seems you should never say never, especially when God might be eavesdropping on your conversation.

I have thought about that conversation many times. In some ways, my thinking hasn't changed. I don't believe in a chess-playing God who moves us into tragedy to teach us a lesson, or get what He wants. But what I have come to believe is that goodness can be found in every situation. That doesn't make every situation good, nor am I belittling the pain and sorrow of hard experiences. What I mean is, in the dark places, light has the biggest impact. When the cloak of darkness feels impenetrable, God is still there. Some of His greatest work is found in the darkness.

Publishing my memoir changed my life; writing it changed me. The healing power of writing has been researched and discussed around the world. Sheryl Sandberg and Adam Grant touch on the power of writing in their book *Option B*. Sheryl's husband unexpectedly died of a heart attack while they were on holiday, leaving her and their two young children. In dealing with her own grief, she wrote in her journal every day because 'turning feelings into words can help us process and overcome adversity'. As Sheryl describes it, 'We all live some form of Option B.'[3] I'm not sure I would call the life I'm living 'Option B'. At times, it feels more like Option W. The problem with our particular version of 'tragedy' is that it doesn't begin with a diagnosis and unfold with time. It isn't a singular event from which to recover. As the parent of a child with a severe disability, things can feel as though they go from bad to worse.

When Sam was ten months old, he began suffering with life-threatening seizures which could go on for over an hour. This means that tucked away alongside memories of my baby sleeping and smiling, I have visions of Tim doing CPR on Sam on our bathroom floor. When Sam was one, we were told it was unsafe to feed him orally and a tube was surgically inserted into his stomach to do the job instead. Shortly after his first birthday, he was registered blind. In our case, instead of time healing, time simply dragged us further and further down the rabbit warren of disability and medical needs.

Today, Sam doesn't have many emergency admissions to hospital, but each day is a complex regime of medicines and 24-hour care, using an electric hoist to lift him from one position to another. Each day I draw up 20 syringes of medication, which are administered eight times a day. Every day: Christmas, his birthday, my birthday, when I'm sick or just plain tired. There is a persistence and relentlessness to caring, which causes a fatigue that penetrates my bones. But alongside the hard work are the most unbelievable highs. The pleasure in simple things like sitting as a family on the sofa watching TV, a walk in the park when everyone is happy, or being snuggled in bed with my son reading a book, are all sweeter because we cherish moments that we might otherwise have taken for granted. The most challenging paths lead to the most beautiful scenery. Often, you simply can't get there any other way.

I've also learnt that 'hard' is not the same as 'bad'. When Sam was younger, I just wanted someone to tell me what life would be like. I wanted to know what else was in store. It is normal for children with disabilities to develop diagnoses as they get older. When milestones are missed and new problems emerge, more bad news is broken; more challenges present themselves. I was tired of being knocked down, picking myself up and being sucker-punched back to the ground once more. But today I'm glad I don't have a crystal ball. I don't know what's in store, and I don't need to. I need to live my life today with the values I hold dear because I don't know what tomorrow will bring.

Tim and I joke that Sam hastened our mid-life crises. Instead of waiting for the next season, when everything would be better, we knew we had to enjoy the now. When Sam started having his life-threatening seizures, we were told that it was unlikely he would live to adulthood. I expect to one day bury my son, but living with that reality changes how I see life, myself and God.

One night, I was in hospital after Sam had a particularly prolonged and severe seizure, when a text from a friend came through suggesting I read 2 Corinthians 4:18: 'So we fix our eyes not on what is seen, but on what is unseen, since what is seen is temporary, but what is unseen is eternal.' My initial response was fury. I thought my friend couldn't possibly understand what I was living through. How could what I was seeing *not* consume me and fill me with fear? But I soon realised I had to focus on what was unseen, because everything in front of my eyes was unpredictable and fragile. As the years have passed, my attitude and prayers have changed. My prayers used to focus on God changing the circumstances of my life, asking Him to 'make this better'; 'give me this opportunity'; or 'fix this situation'. I was largely focused on the circumstances that surrounded me, instead of concentrating on what God was doing within and around me. Gradually, my prayer life changed to ask God to challenge the way I was thinking, my attitude, my heart, and my perspective; always clinging on to the belief of a miraculous God.

When so much was out of my control I realised I needed to work on my own mental health, resilience, rest and community. I knew if I could allow God to nourish my body and mind and transform me in these ways, then everything that was beyond my control would have less of an impact – or at least I would have a greater ability to cope. So I abandoned 'busy' as a status symbol. I learned to see the concept of Sabbath rest as a commandment. I decided to let go of independence and start treasuring interdependence. I chose to find my tribe and walk through life with them. I had to learn the art of self-care and not letting my children always be top of the pile. (After Sam, Tim and I had two more children.) I learned to hold hard emotions. I also had to recognise that each of these things are values I need to try to live by every day, because my default is naturally the flipside of each one.

In her book *Leaving Church*, Barbara Brown Taylor asks the question: 'What is saving your life right now?'[4] Throughout my journey, the answer has changed. The Facebook version of me might be tempted to say running, or quality time with my three sons. The real me would be more likely admit to chocolate and those moments of quiet when my children aren't home.

There have been many seasons in my life where carving out time to spend in silence has saved me. It was during one such time, nestled in the summerhouse at the bottom of our garden, that I began thinking about Mary. She was a young woman who found herself in a mess. She embarked on a scary and rough ride. When Mary gave birth to Jesus, she was homeless, destitute and starting married life as a refugee in a totally unique situation. If I had been her, I would have felt abandoned by the God I had diligently served. Alone and scared, she must have felt forgotten and distant. Those around her may have thought these hard-luck times were her own doing and demonstrated God's disapproval. In my quiet summerhouse, I saw past the quaint, sterilised nativity and saw a frightened and lost young woman struggling to understand what was happening to her. Without the saintly glow or iconic blue headscarf, I could relate to Mary, her sense of confusion and uncertainty. My life did not reflect my hopes or expectations. I couldn't see purpose, rhyme, nor reason. Sam was living on the brink of death and our family edged perilously along the epilepsy tightrope. Then I realised: it didn't make any sense to Mary either. She couldn't possibly comprehend that in the midst of her difficulties, God was more present than He ever had been. In the centre of her turmoil, through the chaos and heartache, not in spite of it, the history of humankind was changing. I realised if I only saw goodness in the easy times, then I could be missing out on something truly great. Right then, I chose to try to continue down the road of acceptance to hope and freedom, even when it didn't make sense.

From the day of Sam's MRI scan, our prayers changed. We didn't want to spend our lives longing for him to be someone he was not, we wanted to love him well and trust that God knew what He was doing when He created him. I began to recognise that freedom arises from within my circumstances, rather than being dependent on me escaping them. When the psalmist wrote, 'The LORD *is* my shepherd; I shall not want' (Psa. 23:1, NKJV), I interpreted the 'not wanting' as the choice of contentment. This life I'm leading is not the one I expected or hoped. But these days I have come to see that God is in the messy reality of today, as He has been for centuries. And if that is where God is, then that is where I want to be: broken, vulnerable and ready to be transformed.

PART TWO

LEARNING TO BE

CHAPTER 7

BEING IN COMMUNITY

Going into hospital for an operation is a strange and vulnerable experience. You put yourself entirely in the hands of other people, trusting they know how to take care of you. Right from the start, you're stripped of your normal protection (goodbye, clothes!) and unflatteringly arrayed in a flimsy hospital gown that gives you next to no dignity – especially in a light breeze. While a consultant came and drew on my legs to make sure he didn't break the wrong one (the fact that this was even a vague possibility did nothing to calm my already very high anxiety), a nurse took my blood pressure, checked my weight and went through all the other usual observations.

Going through the same operation a second time, I knew roughly what I was about to face pain-wise, and had awful, vivid memories of post-op panic attacks I'd had in the hospital. It hadn't been that long since the aftermath of the first operation, and now we were about to go through it all again. I knew there would be pain, sleepless nights and difficult months ahead. I had stopped asking the 'Why me, God?' questions, but I was still putting a lot of pressure on myself to handle it better this time around. I wanted to be stronger and not get so worn down by everything, at the same time as wanting to set myself a better pace of recovery without rushing back to work too soon.

When I came round from the anaesthetic, the first thing that I realised was that the consultant had his arm around me. Though he had just broken my leg, he was clearly a very kind man who seemed to genuinely care about his patients. My body doesn't respond very well to anaesthetic but even though my head was spinning, I looked down and could see there were only two rings around my leg and not three like last time. It's amazing what will cheer you up in these circumstances – I was so happy that I only had two pins going through my leg and out the other side, and only six pins drilled into my bones!

I had to stay in hospital for seven days, so I saw lots of people come and go on the five-bed ward I was on. Everyone was having different procedures, but one thing's for sure: hospital is a real leveller. We were all dependent on the doctors and nurses. We were all in need. The houses we lived in, the cars we drove, the qualifications we did or didn't have – none of it made any difference in there. Suffering is universal. I couldn't avoid it just because I had an OBE, just like the guy next to me couldn't get out of his surgery because of his Master's degree. We were all broken people with broken bodies that needed fixing. Simple tasks like walking and going to the toilet were very difficult, and sometimes impossible on our own. We had to trust others, and be completely vulnerable with people we didn't know. In a hospital gown, with very little independence, all egos disappear.

I found it hard to sleep at night with the constant beeps from the various machines in the room, the sound and pressure of the venous foot pumps strapped around my right foot and left calf to prevent DVT... not to mention the constant comings and goings of my fellow patients. One night when I just couldn't sleep, desperately wanting to be *anywhere* but lying helplessly in a hospital bed with a metal frame on my leg, I started thinking. Lying there frustrated, in pain and wide awake, I began to reflect on the people I had met that day. First, there was Henry, who had been shot and mugged in Nigeria and was wearing a frame like mine as a result. It had already been on for ten months and a recent fall had resulted in one of the pins breaking, so he needed to have it removed and reattached in another painful operation. Because of his injury he hadn't been able to work and had therefore lost his income, but still he stayed positive. Every day, Henry would phone his mum and speak with such tenderness and gratitude for all she had done for him. I found it inspiring that despite the many setbacks he'd faced, he was still so positive.

Then Emmanuel came to mind, the man who served the food on our ward and took such pleasure in his job. Rather than just deliver the trays and walk out again, he tried to make everyone laugh to brighten up their day. When he brought the tea trolley round to our bay, he would muster his highest pitched voice and say, 'There is tea in the house, my friends!' He never failed to make people smile. When Diane and I were chatting with the specialist limb reconstruction nurse, she told us that Emmanuel was just as important to the hospital as the consultant: 'If people are hungry, they will not recover,' she said. 'Every person working here is a cog in a machine; we need all the cogs for the machine to keep working properly.'

That's true for the hospital, and it's true in the bigger picture of the world. We all need one another. Each of us has a part to play, and no one is more or less important to God. All of us are made in His image; each of us is known and cared for. We can so easily put certain people on pedestals, but God sees things so differently: people who are outcast or looked down on by society always have a special place in His heart.

ONE ANOTHER

In his book *Vanishing Grace*, Philip Yancey notes that the phrase 'one another' appears 29 times in various forms in the New Testament, and here are just a few:

Love one another.

Forgive one another.

Pray for one another.

Bear one another's burdens.

Be devoted to one another.

Regard one another as more important than yourself.

Do not speak against one another.

Show tolerance for one another.

Be kind to one another.

Speak truth to one another.

Build up one another.

Comfort one another.

Care for one another.

Stimulate one another towards love and good deeds.[1]

We are made for relationship; connection; community. This isn't always easy, but it's reassuring to know that whatever we have been through, someone else has been through too. We are not on our own, and we have more in common than we realise. We all have doubts, fears and worries – wherever we live in the world, however young or old we are, whatever we do for a living, whether we have great faith or no faith – we all share these common human traits. Yet we're often guilty of assuming that we are the only ones: surely, *no one* else could possibly understand what we're facing, right?

The prophet Elijah can relate. After the epic showdown at Carmel where he called down the fire of God, there was a contract placed on Elijah's life by the queen. He fled and went into hiding, exhausted, depressed, anxious and isolated. We read in 1 Kings 19:4 that he had reached breaking point:

> *'He came to a broom bush, sat down under it and prayed*
> *that he might die. "I have had enough, LORD," he said.*
> *"Take my life".'*

This passage shows us such a beautiful example of how God treats us when we are at our lowest. Elijah was crushed by disappointment, but God didn't tell him to cheer up, or berate him for losing faith. He didn't remind him of the great victory that had just been won and question why that wasn't enough for Elijah. He didn't make him recall previous miracles and find inspiration there. He didn't try to tell him better days were ahead if he would just keep going. Instead, God sent an angel to care for him tenderly, providing him with food so that he would have the strength for the rest of his journey. Elijah was exhausted; he didn't need a pep talk, he needed compassion.

When God speaks, He asks a simple, gentle question:

'What are you doing here, Elijah?' **(1 Kings 19:9)**

To which the prophet replies:

'I have been very zealous for the LORD God Almighty. The Israelites have rejected your covenant, torn down your altars, and put your prophets to death with the sword. I am the only one left, and now they are trying to kill me too.'
(1 Kings 19:10)

Yes, Elijah was lonely and overwhelmed. But though he assumed he was the last man standing, he was anything but: there were actually 7,000 others who hadn't bowed down to Baal (1 Kings 19:18). That's 7,000 people who knew how he felt! There may not be contracted killers hot on our heels, but our struggles can often leave us feeling isolated, abandoned and terrified – and totally alone. But the more I have opened up to others and told them about the things that are painful in my life, the more I have discovered just how many others are in the same boat.

MORE ALIKE THAN UNALIKE

Sharing our common humanity and keeping company with one another doesn't mean we always have to agree on every subject. It's possible to disagree and still have good relationships. I used to play football with a bunch of lads, and afterwards we'd go to the pub, debating anything from politics, to religion, to parenting styles – and we'd *disagree* on most of what we talked about! Yet we'd still leave as friends and the following week, despite our differing opinions, we'd still play on the same team. Held together by a common purpose, we would spur each other on so we could all succeed together.

Sometimes in the Church we let so much divide us. It's right for us to be passionate about what we believe and 'speak truth to one another', but that can cause us to focus on where we differ instead of all that we agree on, to the point that we forget to 'show tolerance for one another' and 'be kind to one another'. We lose sight of the fact that we're all one team with the same goal, and we argue among ourselves until we totally lose sight of the bigger picture.

I have had people ask me how I can bring myself to speak at one political party's conference, and to be friends with people from that party. I can see that comments like that usually come from the pain of believing that the party in question has created structures that cause the poor to suffer. I understand that differing political opinions can seem poles apart, but I've always believed that our voice can be heard louder through building relationships with people we don't see eye to eye with, rather than disengaging with them altogether. Wouldn't it be amazing if our love for each other and our communities spoke so loudly that people outside of the Church couldn't help but ask why? I have chosen to speak to anyone from any political party on issues of injustice, just as I have chosen to pray for our leaders, regardless of whether or not I agree with them.

Moaning on the sidelines doesn't bring positive change; we have to put aside our differences and get involved for the sake of the greater good.

THE LONELINESS EPIDEMIC

Having given many talks on the subject of pain and suffering, I've found that one of the most common responses from people is what I describe as the 'Me too' moment. It's the moment you hear something that tells you that you are not alone, that someone else has experienced what you're going through and shares your struggles. It usually involves someone being willing to be vulnerable and talk not only about the success stories, but the challenges as well. It involves going against the built-in self-preservation mode that tries to shield us from other people's judgments of who we are. Theology and psychology professor John Powell put it like this: 'I am afraid to tell you who I am because you might not like me and that is all that I have to give to you.'[2] Our natural instinct might be to keep people at a distance, afraid that if we let them close they will have the ability to hurt us. We develop self-protective strategies:

> 'The human personality becomes adept at finding ways to relate to people with our real self hidden from view. We develop ways to compensate; we become people pleasers, attention seekers, workaholics, perfectionists, clowns and victims, experts in the art of camouflage.'[3]

When journalist Johann Hari was researching depression, he found that alongside basic physical needs (food, water, shelter), we also have basic psychological needs, including the need to belong. He concluded that 'we have become disconnected from things we really need, and this deep disconnection is driving this epidemic of depression and anxiety all around us.' He also quoted another professor who said, 'being acutely lonely is as stressful as being punched in the face by a stranger – and massively increases your risk of depression.'[4] Other research has indicated that 'the effect of loneliness is equivalent to smoking 15 cigarettes a day and can significantly increase the risk of premature death,[5] while more than three-quarters of GPs see between one and five lonely people a day. Every day. And those are just the ones who are reaching out for help. In a world where technology can help us stay more connected than ever before, we are still unfulfilled in our basic human need to be fully present with one another. We can't seem to go past superficial relationships to ones that give life to us.

I believe we need to let go of the harmful notion that there are 'those in need' and 'those able to help'. We are all in need in some way, and we can all help others. Having needs doesn't make us 'needy'. We will all have times when we feel weak, and times when we feel strong. Let's stop placing judgments on each other's coping mechanisms. For example, why is it OK to admit we've had a huge bar of chocolate because we're feeling low, but not OK to talk about the fact that a bad day led to self-harm? We all have different struggles, and we all find our broken ways to cope. We're not called to judge or to rescue one another, but to be alongside and love one another.

THE VALUE OF EMPATHY

After both of my surgeries, I don't think we would have coped as a family if it weren't for the support of others. Our church arranged people to cook for us, cut our grass, and even walk the dog, which made a huge difference to our daily stresses. Friends who knew I couldn't have visitors for more than a few minutes still made the effort to pop in and say hello. It really helped having people who were consistent. Having an operation is a bit like having a baby in that you initially have lots of visitors, but that tails off over time. When the recovery period takes a while, it can feel like other people's lives soon go back to normal while you're left feeling out of sight and out of mind.

From an emotional point of view, I wasn't looking for anyone to offer any answers as to *why* I was dealing with the things I was. I had heard and thought through every possible theory as to whether it was my fault, or whether God was trying to teach me something; whether it was a hereditary curse or my own lack of faith. I had repented of every sin I could think of, just in case. I didn't need answers. I just wanted people to be with me in my pain and my anxiety. I needed people to love and accept me, even with my doubts.

Brené Brown gives a brilliant short talk on empathy, where she explains how empathy drives connection, while sympathy drives disconnection. She points out that trying to offer a solution or silver-line someone else's problem (eg 'Sorry about the miscarriage but at least you've got children already'; 'Shame you lost your job but at least you got redundancy money') only makes things worse, causing greater pain and disconnection. Empathy, however, is about understanding someone else's perspective, and acknowledging that their perspective is truth for them. It's choosing not to judge someone, and feeling *with* them instead of *for* them: 'Rarely can a response make something better. What makes something better is connection.'[6] The greatest empathic responses come when we acknowledge the pain in ourselves that allows us to relate to what someone else is going through.

Some people can't seem to help but give their opinion, and to my embarrassment, I think I used to be one of them (before I had to have surgery). Now I know what a gift it is to have people who don't try and offer answers, but will be just be there. We see in the book of Job how his friends only piled on the pain during his time of suffering by constantly trying to find a reason for it all. For some of us, the temptation is to try to solve other people's problems with practical solutions. There may be a place for practical advice, but what we most often need is to simply be heard. As Samuel Wells says:

> *'"Being with" is not fundamentally about finding solutions, but about companionship amid struggle and distress. Sometimes the obsession with finding solutions can get in the way of forming profound relationships... and sometimes those relationships are more significant than solutions.'*[7]

When you feel that someone listens and tries to understand you without judgment or needing to move the conversation on, it can be healing in itself. When you're constantly offered solutions, it can make you feel like you're at fault; that if you would only take action, your problems would be solved. Sometimes we just need to listen and allow each other to be heard because, truthfully, we don't usually have solutions anyway. Following a meeting I've led, people sometimes come up and tell me their stories; I see hope in their eyes that I might have some advice, when all I can do is pray and cry with them. As Romans 12:15 says, we 'mourn with those who mourn'. Sitting with people in their grief may be uncomfortable but it can offer comfort and strength, even without us saying a word. When we are willing to enter into the pain of a suffering friend, we follow the example of Jesus, who came to bear our pain and suffer in our place.

CHAPTER 8

BEING LOVED

At our core, we're all seeking to be loved for who we are. We want to know that despite our weaknesses and faults, we are still loveable.

But many of us have learned to look for love in the wrong places: we feel judged on how we perform at school, how good we are at sports, what kind of job we get, and so on, and we get a completely messed up sense of what we're worth. Some of us live with an underlying feeling of being unworthy of love. We think that there is something so fundamentally wrong with us that we don't deserve the love, acceptance and grace that other people do. This internal belief system can affect our relationship with others; we can start to become what we think others want us to be; we act differently around different people, keeping our true selves hidden. We only let people get so close because we don't want them to see behind the illusion we've created. We long for people's approval so we avoid conflict at all costs, even when it's damaging to us. We don't want to offend anyone so we become people pleasers, constantly doing what they want us to do, regardless of whether it's in line with our values. We lose sight of our own needs and operate from a place of exhaustion, constantly giving and giving and feeling like it's never enough.

We feel shame, which causes us to hide, and try to keep anyone from knowing who we really are. It's only when we're completely alone that we feel a sense of relief because then we can finally let go of the need to impress. What an exhausting way to live – all because we don't grasp that we're loveable just as we are.

If we base our self-worth on what others think of us, we'll always be thrown about like a leaf in the wind. Someone will laugh at our jokes, tell us we look beautiful or praise the work we've done and, for a moment at least, we're on top of the world. But the minute we're criticised or something doesn't go quite right, we crash back down. The highs are only temporary.

For many of us, it's the ridiculously high standards we set for ourselves that allow the lies to creep in and whisper that we're not good enough. As we've already seen, shame loves a perfectionist. Perfectionism convinces us that nothing less than 100% will do and labels us a failure when we can't meet the standard. It makes us rake over mistakes from the past, torturing ourselves when there's nothing we can do to change them. Even when we do excel, the perfectionist tendency is to put success down to other people and miss out a feeling of accomplishment. For a perfectionist, the feeling of not being worthy remains no matter what.

If we want to know how loved we are, we need to know to whom we belong.

A PRODIGAL GOD

It's easy to switch off when people start talking about the parable of the prodigal son (Luke 15). The story is so famous and so familiar that we can assume we've heard it all before. Growing up, I mostly heard this parable preached as an evangelistic sermon, but I just couldn't relate to it. I was one of those kids who never went off the rails. I didn't join a gang, didn't do drugs, didn't carry a weapon and I didn't even get drunk, so I didn't think this story was relevant to me. Over the years I've discovered there is so much more to it than I originally thought.

It's not entirely uncommon in this day and age for older parents to pass on some of their savings to their children while they are alive (though most people would still consider it pretty rude for a child to ask for it!). But in first-century Palestine, the younger son asking for his inheritance early was the equivalent of him saying, 'Dad, I wish you were dead.' People listening to Jesus would have expected the father to react to this painful insult by telling his son to leave and never come back.

If you're a parent and you've ever had your child tell you they hate you, you'll know how gutting it is. Even when you can handle it rationally and know they are just upset, it still hurts to hear those words from your own child, who you would do anything for. In the past I've been tempted to respond by reminding my kids of all I do for them and telling them they should be grateful, but the father in this story takes a different tack. He humbly grants the son's request. He doesn't seek to control him or talk him out of what he must know will be a venture that won't end well. He has the wisdom to realise that if his son is at the point of asking something so life-defining, which would bring serious dishonour to the family, he can only let him go and make his own mistakes. But it's not as if the father in this parable had money sitting in an ISA waiting to be retrieved; he would have had to sell his land to give the son his inheritance. Jesus' listeners would have been astonished. The father should beat the son and kick him out for being so disrespectful and betraying his family and community, not go out of his way to do as he asked! Already we see the difference between our human hearts and God's Father heart.

The point in the story where the son leaves home is right about where I used to switch off, thinking the preacher was just trying to warn me that if I developed a taste for wild living, I'd be eating with the pigs. Then I read Henri Nouwen's book, *The Return of the Prodigal Son*, and this really rang true for me:

> 'I am the prodigal son every time I search for unconditional love where it cannot be found. Why do I keep ignoring the place of true love and persist in looking for it elsewhere? Why do I keep leaving home where I am called a child of God, the Beloved of my Father? I am constantly surprised at how I keep taking the gifts God has given me – my health, my intellectual and emotional gifts – and keep using them to impress people, receive affirmation and praise, and compete for rewards, instead of developing them for the glory of God. Yes, I often carry them off to a "distant country" and put them in the service of an exploiting world that does not know their true value.'[1]

If we look for security anywhere except in our heavenly Father's love, eventually we will realise that nothing else can satisfy. When the son loses all his money and ends up taking a job as a pig farmer (pigs being disgusting and 'unclean' to a Jewish audience), he decides his best strategy is to head home, tail between his legs, and try to convince his dad to hire him instead. He's hit rock bottom.

In normal family life in this era, the mother would be the one to meet the returning son while the father stayed in the house. In Jesus' story, however, we see the father looking out for him, waiting expectantly. The son would have known, as would the crowds listening to Jesus, that what followed next should have been a *kezazah* ceremony (to signify one being 'cut off' from the community or family). The villagers would break a pot on the floor at the son's feet as a sign that his relationship with them was broken. They would shout, bringing shame and humiliation on the returning son, and as a community they would publicly reject him. Knowing what the community would be ready to do, the father had to get to his son first. He would have hitched up his tunic and run – something respectable men never did in that culture. It would have been considered completely undignified, shameful and humiliating. Yet that was the father's response! He didn't want his son to experience the humiliation and rejection of the *kezazah*, so he humiliated himself instead to save him. This is a beautiful picture of what God did for us on the cross: He was humiliated and shamed in our place so that we don't need to be.

The prodigal son didn't even get to deliver the grovelling speech he'd rehearsed in the pigpen and all the way home. Before he could say a word, stutter an apology or try to make amends, the grace and the love of his father overwhelmed him. We can come to God ready to defend ourselves, or prepare long speeches on how sorry we are, when He is already eager to show us His love and grace. Grace is unmerited love and favour; by definition, we can't earn it.

The massive celebration that concludes the parable isn't for the prodigal son. On his blog, The Reverend Doctor Daniel DeForest London comments:

> 'No-one in the village would attend a party held in honour of such a disrespectful son. The celebration honours the father and the father's self-sacrifice and generosity in restoring his son's family. The father sacrificed his social dignity and broke the patriarchal code in order to save his son. It is saving and sacrificial love of the father that the banquet celebrates.'[2]

Many of us can relate to the elder son in this story. He hasn't messed up, he's served faithfully, so he doesn't understand why his reckless younger brother is being so richly rewarded after the shame he's brought on the family. He's so angry he describes his brother to his dad as 'this son of yours' (Luke 15:30). He accuses his brother of sleeping with prostitutes, and refuses to attend his father's celebration. But in doing so, he effectively insults his father in a similar way to the son who left home. Once again, the father has every right to put his foot down and demand that his eldest son attend the party or be punished. Surely there is only so much hurt and embarrassment a man can take? But he realises the elder son is just as lost as the younger. He didn't seek love in a faraway land with women and wine, but he did seek it through trying to earn his father's approval. That's why many have suggested this parable should be called 'the lost *sons*'.

The elder son protested to his father, 'All these years I've been slaving for you'. Have you ever been tempted, in times of pain and discouragement, to say to God, 'It's not fair. I've been trying really hard to follow You faithfully and serve You, and I'm suffering while other people seem to walk through life without a care in the world.' Sometimes we get so busy working *for* God that we miss out on intimacy *with* God. When we get our affirmation from what we do, we are trying to earn God's love. We are lost. We've 'left home', and our eyes are no longer fixed on our loving Father. Both sons were lost, trying to find fulfilment in different ways, but Jesus' story only tells us about how things turned out for the younger son. We know that he came home and was restored, but we're left guessing as to whether or not the elder son could humble himself and accept the father's love and grace too.

WHERE IS GOD?

Of course, during times of pain, it can be especially hard to hold on to the truth that we're loved. Many of our 'why' questions have at their heart the deeper questions: 'Do You love me, God?' 'Where are You, God?'

On my last birthday, Diane and I went to Auschwitz. I know this might sound strange – most people choose to go for dinner or to the theatre– but this was something I had always wanted to do. As you walk the tour around the death camp, no one speaks. There are no words to describe the horror and sadness you can sense in a place where over a million people lost their lives. At the end of the tour I asked our guide, 'What happens to a person's faith in a place like this?' He replied, 'You lose it, or it sustains you.' In his book, *Night*, Elie Wiesel records the true story of the child who was hanged from the gallows alongside two fellow prisoners. The rest of the camp had to troop past the hanging bodies, and Wiesel describes how, though the two other men died instantly, the young child was too light for the rope to snap his neck, and hovered between life and death. As they watched someone groaned:

> *"'For God's sake, where is God?"*
> *And from within me, I heard a voice answer: "Where is He? This is where – hanging here from this gallows."'*[3]

I stood with the guide in front of the gallows, and the reality of the truth hit me again: God is not removed from our pain. He suffers with us. He can be trusted, even in the midst of utter horror. It's not always easy to remember. Many of us live in a place similar to the disciples on Easter Saturday: they've seen the brutality of the cross crushing their Lord, their hopes, their dreams, and are yet to know the healing joy of the resurrection that is to come. We don't know how our lives will turn out. We don't know which situations God will turn around in miraculous ways, and for which He will offer His comfort until we know true freedom in heaven. We are trusting in love; we are trusting in something bigger and more beautiful than ourselves. I have many questions, but even when I'm struggling with them, I cannot deny that God is love.

LEARNING TO LIVE LOVED

Sometimes I wish I could say a magic prayer and find that I am 100% secure in God's love. No matter how many sermons we hear, or times we read it in the Bible, or all the ways God shows us, we still lose sight of this incredible love. Living loved means rejecting the lies that tell us we are only worthy of love if we achieve something. It's constantly reminding ourselves that every time we go into a potential conflict situation or receive criticism, our self-esteem doesn't have to be on the table; it doesn't have to fluctuate according to what anyone else thinks. We are loved, enjoyed and liked by God. We need to build a resilience that allows us to listen to other people's approval and criticism of us without letting it define us.

This isn't a book of simple answers because these are complex questions. The reasons you may struggle to feel loved are likely to be different to the reasons why I struggle, especially when we're talking about the painful experiences of the past. But God's love is not conditional. Wherever you are at, you are a masterpiece. You are fearfully and wonderfully made by Almighty God, and He thinks you're worth dying for. I pray that you would know that love in a new and deeper way now; and on the days when you don't feel loved, I pray that you will trust that it is still true, regardless. Paul's words to the Romans are categorical here:

> 'For I am convinced that neither death nor life, neither
> angels nor demons, neither the present nor the future, nor
> any powers, neither height nor depth, nor anything else in
> all creation, will be able to separate us from the love of God
> that is in Christ Jesus our Lord.' **(Rom. 8:38–39)**

Were he writing today, Paul might add, 'neither depression,
nor anxiety, nor self-harm; neither cancer nor OCD nor an
eating disorder; no pain from the past or the present or the
future; no disappointment or shattered dream, can stop God
from loving us.'

LOVING OTHERS

Nouwen's commentary on the prodigal son is to highlight
that whether you identify with the younger son or the elder,
you need to realise that you are also called to be the father.
The father models what the Church is called to do: to love
unconditionally, to forgive even when we've been hurt, and
to show compassion, grace and mercy to a hurting and broken
world. We're not to be people who crave status and control,
keen to feed our own egos. We need to love without the need
to receive love or thanks in return; to love without condition
because we feel God's pain for others. This is a picture of our
God who is generous, who loves and forgive us, who wants
to share His joy and show us His mercy. There is no limit to
what God would do for us. Tim Keller points out that the word
'prodigal' means 'recklessly extravagant meaning having
spent everything', which is why Keller describes God as 'the

prodigal God'.[4] He gave everything for us, and when we give to others extravagantly, we reflect something of His nature.

I can't help but be inspired by Dominique Voillaume, a priest who lived in a poor neighbourhood in Paris. At the age of 54, he was dying of inoperable cancer. Early every morning, he would go to a park to hang out with the local drifters, drunks, has-beens and dirty old men who looked at the girls walking by. He never criticised, judged or reprimanded them – he simply told stories, shared his food and accepted them with unconditional love. When they asked Dominique to tell them about his life, he was able to share God's love and tell them that God had come for those who, like them, had been rejected by society and were outcasts. His witness was credible because he was living it out and the group of people he spent time with began to change. After Dominique had shared Jesus with them in such a beautiful way, one guy said, 'the dirty jokes, vulgar language and leering at girls just stopped.' When Dominique died, his journal was found and it contains the key to how he lived. His last entry is one of the most amazing things I have ever read:

'All that is not the love of God has no meaning for me. I can truthfully say that I have no interest in anything but the love of God which is in Christ Jesus. If God wants it to, my life will be useful through my word and witness. If he wants it to, my life will bear fruit through my prayers and sacrifices. But the usefulness of my life is his concern, not mine. It would be indecent of me to worry about that.'[5]

More than seven thousand people attended his funeral. A more humble and yet fruitful life would be hard to find. Dominique knew he was loved. He found that God's love is more precious than anything else we will ever discover. Once he had grasped that, his life naturally overflowed to loving others. In a culture so obsessed with popularity (virtual or otherwise), to be concerned only with what God thinks of us really goes against the grain. To have no interest in anything but the love of God, and how that love is being reflected through us, is a huge challenge.

I want to grasp God's love for me in the same way that Dominique Voillaume did. I want to hold on to the truth of that love in the good and bad times. I want to understand deep down in my soul that God doesn't expect me to be perfect – He knows my weakness, He knows my struggles and His love for me is not changed one iota by them. His love for me is not dependent on me or what I do, it is solely dependent on Him and He never changes. I want this love to shape how I see myself and how I see the rest of the world. I want to spend the rest of my life going to those who feel forgotten, who feel like God has abandoned them – not because I think it will earn me points in heaven, but because God's love flows through me so profoundly that there's no possible way I could keep that love to myself.

JOHN'S STORY

I first met John many years ago when we came up with a crazy idea of turning a police riot van into a mobile recording studio. At the time, John was a police superintendent and I was running XLP. We went together to pitch our van idea to MTV as part of their *Pimp My Ride* programme. To our surprise they said yes, and it became the most watched programme on MTV that year. Most importantly, that's how we then had a van that could be used to go on estates across London to engage with some of the hardest-to-reach young people. Since that moment, John has become one of my best friends. When I am having a down day, John is one of the first people I text asking for prayer. He always replies with, 'Go gently', reminding me to give myself a break. John has been one of those friends who has blessed me hugely in my journey, and it's been a privilege to walk with him through some of what he's about to tell you.

I think I was about five years old when I first realised it was my job to look after everyone else. No one told me I needed to; it wasn't even a conscious thought. I was just a small boy reacting to circumstances.

I remember standing under the glare of the strip lights in a hospital corridor at St Bart's, holding my mum's hand while my three-year-old sister was in theatre. She had been diagnosed with retinal blastoma – a horrible form of cancer – and was having surgery to remove her eye. I didn't have the knowledge or the language to understand what was going on, but I knew that it was serious – life and death serious. I decided I needed to do what I could to make sure everyone else was OK. I squeezed mum's hand and tried to reassure her, saying, 'Don't worry. Everything is going to be alright.' The surgery saved my sister's life and she went on to make a wonderful recovery, but these things leave their mark.

My dad left the family home when I was 17 and I was shattered by his departure. By default, I had become the man of the house and my deep sense of responsibility for my mum and two younger sisters only increased over time. If not me, then who would take care of them?

Perhaps those two events played a part in my aspiration to become a police officer. It was the only job I ever wanted to do, the only application form I ever filled out, the only interview I ever went for. I had no interest in following my dad by being a vicar in the Church of England, or my mum by being a teacher. I knew I didn't want to be stuck behind a desk in an office – I wanted to be a boy in blue.

If you ask most police officers why they joined, they will simply tell you that they wanted to make a difference. The fact that it's a well-worn phrase doesn't make it any less true. I'm not sure I could honestly claim that as my only motivation – at least, not at the start. I was also looking for adventure, for belonging, for the opportunity to be a part of something bigger than me and, of course, for the chance to drive on the wrong side of the road at 90mph, sirens sounding and blue lights blazing.

As I was preparing to join the police, I had an interesting

conversation with the youth leader from my church. He suggested to me that I could be a Christian or a policeman, but I couldn't be both. That just didn't make sense to me. As far as I could see, being a policeman was a great way to love my neighbour in the way that Jesus asked, serving those who are vulnerable and in need. What better place to try to shine a bit of God's light and love?

I loved my police training: 20 weeks at Hendon, followed by two years out on the streets, learning the ropes. My first posting after leaving training school was a quiet one based in Central London, but after a couple of years I transferred to Brixton, and everything changed. Policing became every bit the adventure I thought it would be. I loved everything about the job, not least the colleagues I served with. They were some of the funniest and most mischievous people I'd ever met, their humour and comradery offering welcome relief from the inevitable challenges of the job. I've never been one to dispute some of the criticism that gets levelled at the police; we're by no means perfect. But it's an extraordinary thing to work day in, day out alongside colleagues who are willing to put themselves in harm's way in defence of complete strangers. It has been my privilege to work with some of the most inspiring, courageous and compassionate people you could ever hope to meet.

I was utterly naïve when I started out. I was in no way street-wise, and that became apparent when I was first called to a pub fight. I was bewildered by the violence, as grown men relentlessly threw punches at one another. As I jumped in, the epaulette on the shoulder of my uniform was torn off. I had never encountered anything remotely like it before, but I wanted to be wherever the action was. I think there was a big part of me that wanted to prove myself, and show that I was worthy of being an officer. I wanted to be liked by those I worked alongside, so I didn't shy away from anything that needed doing and was quick to volunteer for any task.

I hadn't been in Brixton long before I attended my first murder scene. I'd seen dead bodies before – people who had died in non-suspicious circumstances – but this was different. It was a domestic murder: a young woman had been stabbed repeatedly in the throat. I was the first officer on the scene. Back then, there was no preparation before you went, and no one would ask how you were afterwards. It was just part and parcel of the job. You don't have time to prepare yourself either – the call comes, and you have to go.

My first murder scene was followed swiftly by another, and so began many years of dealing with some of the most horrific situations imaginable. At the start, although much of it was shocking, I was resilient and the adrenalin of being in these situations carried me through. To a large extent I was carried along on the extraordinary adventure of it all. If anything, I sought out these experiences. I wanted to go when the calls came; I wanted to be there to do what I could. It's part of the instinct of a police officer.

There's no such thing as a regular day, week or month when you're a copper. That's part of the appeal. One day you might be at the scene of a fatal crash; another day, you're called to a home where there's been a cot death; yet another day, you're negotiating during an armed siege. You might be the first on the scene of a stabbing, dealing with armed and violent men, or telling distraught parents their child has been killed. Those things don't necessarily happen every day, but they are common enough. Again and again, you see the very worst that human beings are capable of. You witness people's moments of trauma, the worst days of their lives, and all you can do is try to make a difference.

I didn't ever feel like I was making a conscious effort to suppress my feelings, but subconsciously I was tucking them away so I could get on with the job in hand. Most people never encounter in their whole lives the sorts of horror we deal with on a weekly or even daily basis. The most common reaction to stories we tell is disbelief. Yet for those who work in these areas, it's just part of the job. There's a certain natural distance that you place between yourself and your emotions, and what's happening in front of you. If you sat and cried over every crime scene, you'd never be able to get your job done. And, of course, some of the things you encounter make great tales to tell. It's part of the adventure – sharing stories and watching people's mouths drop open in amazement. Strangers would hang on your every word as you spoke about a world they had little comprehension of beyond the works of fiction.

Through the years I have worked in a variety of ranks and roles within the Metropolitan Police, from constable through to chief superintendent. I have loved almost every moment of it. But, during that time, I've also seen some alarming developments in society: increases in violent crime; in the levels of harm inflicted; in the speed at which incidents escalate; in the vulnerability of those who are targeted; in the sense of hopelessness that characterises too many households and neighbourhoods. Patrick and I share a passionate concern for the young people in London who are caught up in serious violence and knife crime. It is one of the most pressing issues of our time. And I have stood in far too many of the haunted places where the lives of children have been lost. I'm troubled by the apparent normalisation of violence in society; by the rise of sexual offences; by the unfettered availability of extreme pornography on the internet; by what some young men appear to expect; by what some young women appear to accept; I'm troubled by the loss of innocence. I'm troubled by human trafficking, by the exploitation of children, by the 'county lines' drugs trade (the movement of drugs from inner-city hubs to out-of-town locations) and by the relentless persistence of domestic violence – the single greatest cause of harm in society. I'm troubled by it all.

Looking back, I can begin to understand the extent to which policing can take its toll. Little by little, your resilience gets eaten into. Each time, it gets a little harder to get on with the job in hand without being overwhelmed by the sheer horror of it all. When you're working in an environment where this sort of thing is the norm, you build a kind of resistance to it but, inevitably, things get through. Faced with the trauma of frontline policing, the natural, normal, healthy thing is to feel; for the broken lives and broken bones to break your heart. But for years, I tucked it all away in my subconscious and just got on with the job.

Then everything changed.

In February 2013, after more than 20 years as a police officer, I went to California for a week to spend time with friends and visit their church. I had just moved from being the borough commander of Camden to the same role in Southwark. It was a job I loved, but it was hugely demanding and I wanted to take a bit of time and space to think, pray and plan before heading back into the madness. On my forty-third birthday, I was standing in the church auditorium. It was the end of the formal part of the service but the band was still playing. And, without any kind of warning, something just snapped in the back of my head. I had no idea what it was, but it was terrifying. My mind immediately started to cloud over and I felt as though I was losing my grip on the world around me. But I didn't say a word to anyone. I didn't have the words to explain.

I flew back to London the next day as planned, and the return to my family and to my role at Southwark seemed to ease things a little. I told Bear (my wife) what had happened, but then set it to one side. I had a job to do. I didn't understand that I was seriously ill – and that I was getting worse. I became absolutely overwhelmed with exhaustion. I just couldn't shake it off. Having been a police officer for so long, I was used to being tired. And with three kids under the age of ten, I told myself that tiredness was just a fact of life. *Get on with it, man.* Then the exhaustion was compounded by anxiety. I'd been anxious many times before – on my wedding day, before the birth of our first child, when I was being assessed for promotion – but this was entirely different. It was malevolent and utterly overwhelming. I'd wake up in the middle of the night, completely gripped by panic but with no idea why. I limped on, still not understanding, still not asking for help at work, still not realising that I was sick.

And then came the depression.

I'm not sure where to even begin to find the words to describe what depression is like. In truth, I suspect that only those who have been there can ever fully understand. Depression is a thing of raw horror and blind terror; a waterboarding of the mind. It is a suffocating, silent agony that reduced me to rubble. Depression is the thief of joy and hope. It robs you of the ability to find any form of joy today. It takes from you the capacity to feel any sort of hope for tomorrow.

Finally, I knew that I was broken (though I still didn't realise how badly). I decided that I would take two weeks off work. Even that seemed like a big deal to me. I had only missed a total of five days in the whole of the previous decade, and surely a fortnight would be enough to be able to get back on my feet. But it was just the beginning of my fall.

I felt the sharp sting of shame: the shame of not being strong enough; of stumbling; of not being there for my colleagues; of being at home while they continued to take the calls; of not being the husband or the dad I wanted to be. And, in my ignorance and confusion, I felt the shame of mental illness. I was a crumpled, frightened shadow, huddled on the sitting room floor. In the end, I was off work for more than seven months and, even then, only able to return to work on a very limited basis. Throughout it all, Bear was extraordinary: calm, kind, patient, strong. Remarkable in every possible way. She was, and is, the very best thing that ever happened to me. My colleagues also responded magnificently. Many recognised that what had happened to me could just as easily happen to them, and they did all they could to support me.

For the first three months, I was in a very bad way. I

managed to get myself out of bed each day but was able to do little more than lie quietly on the sofa, breathing in and out. I couldn't think about much more than getting through the day, until the next sleeping pill was due and I could block the world out for a few hours. The religious certainty I'd grown up with failed me completely. For six months, I didn't make it to church. I couldn't read my Bible and I could barely string together a sentence of prayer. There was no Christian platitude that was going to fix me. All that remained was a single, simple fragment from Psalm 46: 'Be still and know that I am God.' And that was it. That was all I had. I would whisper it quietly to myself. I had nothing to give God, but as the days drifted painfully slowly, I began to catch a faint glimpse – perhaps for the very first time in my life – of what grace might be. I began to question myself: 'Can I lie here and say nothing and read nothing and do nothing, and that be enough?' I was used to being capable and confident at work, proving my worth by what I did. And it finally dawned on me that, throughout my life, I had been trying to earn God's approval by being a 'good Christian'. So how could this simple scrap of the Old Testament, which was all I had to offer, be enough? But, gloriously, it was. It was enough. In fact, I didn't even need the verse. I was enough. I am enough just as I am.

Though I had nothing to give God, He still loved me. It didn't matter that I wasn't at church, that I wasn't able to read my Bible or form a coherent prayer. All that mattered was that I was loved. I lay there because I could do no more than lie there; I offered nothing because I had nothing to offer, and yet it made not one jot of difference to God's love for me. By grace I began to understand grace – the rumour that I am loved beyond measure, just as I am.

We in the Church can be just as bad as the rest of the world at believing that we are what we achieve. We're measured by our job title, our salary potential, our number of Twitter followers, the speed we can run a 10k. Our performance-orientated culture constantly places us in a league table where we're ranked better than or worse than the person next to us. We've lost the ability to just be, and for that to be enough.

While all of this was happening, I was getting some practical help too. My doctor prescribed anti-depressants and he referred me for emergency counselling. I accepted both without hesitation. Apart from anything else, I was desperate.

Gradually, the worst of the depression began to subside. It's important to acknowledge that medication doesn't work for everyone, but it works for me – and I will take it for as long as I need to. Why wouldn't I? A few years ago, one of my sisters had her thyroid removed. As a consequence, her body no longer produces the thyroxine that it needs. But, thanks to the wonder of modern medical miracles, she is able to take a single tablet each day, which makes up for what is missing. Why should it be any different with my head?

I suspect that we could all do with seeing a counsellor or psychologist from time to time too. It's always been good to talk. Anna, my psychologist, and I talked about life and about work. We talked about sorrow and joy; about the past and the present; about the faces and the places that had seared themselves into my soul. We began to disentangle me – and put me back together. I still see her now.

There remains a stigma in society about mental ill health

– caused, I suppose, by a combination of fear and a lack of understanding. And that needs to change. I'm not ashamed anymore: not of the meds I take; not of the counselling I need; not of the story of the last few years of my life. It's a part of who I am. One of most beautiful descriptions of Jesus in the Bible is as 'a man of suffering, and familiar with pain' (Isa. 53:3), but I've never heard a sermon about that. Someone ought to preach it. Because we all have our stories and we all have our scars.

You could offer me all the treasures of this world and I wouldn't volunteer to repeat the experience of falling – but neither would I choose to give up all that has happened as a consequence. There have been endless silver linings. The extraordinary love of my wife (everyone ought to marry a no-nonsense North Yorkshire farmer's daughter); the unexpected hours and days spent with my three beautiful girls; the faithfulness of friends and the kindness of strangers; the time and space to think and breathe – and to begin to learn how to rest in a fast-moving world; the discovery of writing and of the healing to be found in the telling of stories; the opportunity to stand up and speak up for the things that matter more; the discovery of those unforced rhythms of grace. But I'm still a work in progress. I'm still a beginner. Society tries to focus on the goal and perpetually pushes us to the point where we can say, 'I've arrived'. But I think God is more interested in the journey. None of us really 'arrives' until we get to heaven. I think He wants us to find companions who will walk alongside us, and He wants us to slow down far more than we're inclined to with our busy lives and list of things we want to achieve. Faith has nothing whatsoever to do with rules, and everything to do with amazing grace. We tend to look for certainty – we want to explain and define and put everything into a neat little box. But you could no more put God in a box than fit the universe on the head of a pin. He is entirely beyond our comprehension. And there's a danger that we have lost the place for wonder and mystery in our lives.

I'm a whole lot better now than I once was, but I need to continue to look after myself. I need to develop what Martin Luther King once described as rational, healthy self-interest. Most of us will have sat through one of those unfathomably dull safety briefings shown before take-off on an aeroplane. I want you to pay closer attention next time – particularly to the part that describes the oxygen masks dropping down from the roof of the plane. The instructions are clear: even if you have a young child sitting next to you, you need to fit your own oxygen mask first. Because your ability to look after anyone else is connected, inextricably, to your ability to look after yourself. Seems like a pretty good metaphor for life. I am learning slowly what that means in practice for me. Friends, family and faith are the things that seem to matter most – and I need to keep making time and space for them. Rest, medication and counselling are the things that seem to help me most in a world that is moving faster than is good for any of us.

But, ultimately, it means being still. And knowing that He is God.

You can read more of John Sutherland's story in his book *Blue: A Memoir – Keeping the Peace and Falling to Pieces* (London: Orion Publishing Group, 2017).

CHAPTER 9

BEING STILL

I've been fortunate enough to visit Ghana many times. Though it is a country I love, I usually spend the first few days I'm there bubbling with frustration. The pace of life is so slow. No one is in a rush to get anywhere or to do anything. 'We'll be there at two,' may as well mean, 'We'll eventually rock up at five.' No one seems to be as worried about the clock as I am, and my used-to-being-busy mindset just cannot deal with it. The more uncomfortable I get, the more I begin to realise that I, like many in our western culture, am addicted to hurry.

Diane and I are constantly trying to work out how to slow our lives down. Not just because it leaves us feeling exhausted when we're running around at 100mph each day, but because being too busy gives people the impression we don't have time for them. People need to know that there is space in our lives for them, not as projects but as individuals who can't be expected to schedule their needs in line with our diaries. We don't want to feel like our relationships operate at a surface level, and the reality is that for any relationship to grow and develop, it needs time. There are no shortcuts.

Sometimes we make time for people from a physical point of view (for example, being home to see the kids before they go to bed), but on an emotional level, our minds are elsewhere. I might be reading *Moose on the Loose* to my son Caleb, and though I'm sitting right beside him, my mind has wandered to thinking about how I can raise enough money for a new charity, when I am going to prepare the talk I need to give next week, which texts have I forgotten to reply to… and so it goes on. I'm there with Caleb, but I'm not sharing the moment and laughing like he is at the moose's antics; I'm rushing through so I can tick the box that I've done the bedtime story and get back to the other things demanding my attention.

Do you experience a similar thing when it comes to your relationship with God? Maybe we whizz through a Bible reading so it's done, rather than taking time to invite the Holy Spirit to speak to us through it. We're attending church but keeping one eye on the clock, thinking about the afternoon ahead. I love how Mike Yaconelli summarises this:

'We're not rejecting God; we just don't have time for him. We've lost him in the blurred landscape as we rush by on our way to church. We don't struggle with the Bible, but with the clock. It's not that we're too decadent, we're too busy. We don't feel guilty because of sin, but because we have no time for our spouse, our children or our God. It's not sinning too much that's killing our souls, it's schedule that's annihilating us. Most of us don't come home at night staggering drunk. Instead we come home staggering tired, worn out, exhausted and drained because we live too fast.' [1]

A friend of mine said that life can sometimes feel like a game of Tetris. I used to be addicted to that as a kid. Do you remember how blocks of different shapes and sizes would fall from the top of the screen and you had to turn them the right way so that when they landed, they made a straight line? When you succeeded, that line disappeared – but more blocks were constantly falling, and you had to be quick enough to move them at the right time into the right place. The more successful you were, the faster the blocks started to come down… until eventually you couldn't get them into lines, they all landed in a jumbled mess, and you lost the game. Anyone else's life ever feel like that?! Things are often coming at us insanely fast and we're desperately trying to prioritise so we don't mess things up.

RUTHLESSLY ELIMINATE HURRY

Author and pastor John Ortberg was mentored by Dallas Willard. In a conversation that had a profound effect on Ortberg's ministry, he asked Willard what he needed to do to stay spiritually healthy. Willard replied, 'Hurry is the great enemy of spiritual life in our day. You must ruthlessly eliminate hurry from your life.'[2] Wow. Many of us struggle to see what we can take out of our days. Most of the sermons I have ever heard preached on the subject of rest and stillness seem to have been written by preachers who live in the mountains and whose children have long since grown up. It would drive me crazy wondering how they suggested I slowed down with a charity to run and four young children needing plenty of attention!

But I've come to realise that the problem for me isn't my work or my family – it's that I always feel like I have to fight for something. Maybe, instead of moving to the mountains, I need to learn to let go of my need for significance. I'm guessing I'm not alone. How many of us are driven by the insecurity of not wanting to let others down? Of needing their affirmation? Of needing to be needed, or of feeling guilty when we say no to someone? How many of us have a fear of failure that keeps us relentlessly pursuing our goals and striving for perfection? Have we made exhaustion a status symbol, or simply allowed it to become a habit that we haven't questioned in many years? Are our daily actions motivated by genuine need, or by fear?

We need to learn to think and act differently and to be intentional about the pace of life we sustain; to perhaps invest in fewer but deeper relationships; to learn strategies to quieten the negative inner dialogue; to be present in the moment and not constantly distracted by our fear. We need to know our own limits (even if our limits are different to other people's) and not push ourselves beyond them. We need to remember that our energy is a precious resource; we don't have to use every ounce of it every day. We need to pace ourselves because we can't run at full-pelt all the time. It's wise to keep some energy in reserve for when a crisis hits or we're in a particularly busy season. If we constantly live at full capacity, adrenalin will carry us through for a while but it's not designed as a long-term solution:

> 'The highs and lows drain us of emotional energy and our
> drivenness leads to exhaustion. With restlessness and

unease in our soul, the weight of weariness takes its toll and life becomes a duty, not a delight.'[3]

Maybe if I accepted myself, even with my weaknesses, maybe if I let go of some of the unhealthy things that drive me, I could learn to be as content as Paul said he was to the Philippians:

'I am not saying this because I am in need, for I have learned to be content whatever the circumstances. I know what it is to be in need, and I know what it is to have plenty. I have learned the secret of being content in any and every situation, whether well fed or hungry, whether living in plenty or in want. I can do all this through him who gives me strength.' **(Phil. 4:11–13)**

BEING IN THE MOMENT

When we talk about slowing down and refocusing in church, the story of Mary and Martha often gets brought up. This is a passage of the Bible that I misunderstood for many years:

'As Jesus and his disciples were on their way, he came to a village where a woman named Martha opened her home to him. She had a sister called Mary, who sat at the Lord's feet listening to what he said. But Martha was distracted by all the preparations that had to be made. She came to him and asked, "Lord, don't you care that my sister has left me to do the work by myself? Tell her to help me!"

"Martha, Martha," the Lord answered, "you are worried

and upset about many things, but few things are needed –
or indeed only one. Mary has chosen what is better, and it
will not be taken away from her.'" **(Luke 10:38–42)**

I used to groan when I heard a preacher start speaking on this story. I knew it would make me feel guilty, because it always seemed to be expounded like this: 'Mary sat at the feet of Jesus, learning from him. Martha was in the kitchen, complaining. Mary is good. Martha is bad. You need to spend more time at the feet of Jesus.'

The more I studied it, the more I realised it wasn't quite that simple. Mary and Martha have different personalities. I find that I identify more with Martha, who likes to be active and get things done, so I can relate to her feeling that Mary isn't pulling her weight with the domestic tasks. If I'm honest, I think Mary would be the sort of person who would have me gritting my teeth and passive-aggressively banging pots and pans to make a point!

Mary is sitting at Jesus' feet, taking everything in. And of course the message we always come away with is that we need to be more like Mary and less like Martha: we need to stop rushing around and just take time to sit at the Lord's feet. But this can be a dangerous message, especially when we're trying to think carefully about our pace of life. In other parts of the Bible, it says it's good to be busy, and there are more warnings against laziness than there are about drunkenness. Jesus Himself was pretty busy a lot of time, and the last thing He said to His disciples was along the lines of, 'Get going and tell everyone about me!' It's dangerous to imply that God cannot be present when we are actively doing things. It creates a dualism and misses the point about allowing Christ into all areas of our lives. It's not necessarily about doing less, but being present in the moment – something I am terrible at. I am always thinking ahead to the next thing and often miss what is going on around me. I struggle to engage with the here and now.

The 'doing versus being' discussion is often what stands out to us in this story, but at the time of Jesus, what was far more shocking was a rabbi entering the home of an unmarried woman (Mary), and her then spending time with Him in an area of the house reserved for the men to meet. In that culture, to sit at someone's feet was a way to indicate the relationship between a disciple and a rabbi. Mary's posture meant she was there to listen and learn, rather than to chill out and avoid the washing up. Through the simple act of just sitting there, Mary was quietly taking her place as someone who wanted to be a teacher and preacher of the kingdom of God – a radical step in such a culture. Perhaps Martha missed out because she hadn't understood what was available to her, there and then.

The point isn't whether we are in the kitchen; it's whether we're present with Jesus. We can easily fall into the trap of engaging with God in 'spiritual activities' such as going to church or a Bible study group, and miss experiencing God in our daily lives. Let's be aware of God's nearness when we're peeling potatoes, when we're studying or working, when we're serving at foodbanks, when we're taking a walk in the woods, or watching the sun set. If we're truly present in the moment, we will know that God is there with us.

AN ATTITUDE OF GRATITUDE

When we learn to be present, gratitude often follows – and that's so beneficial to our mental wellbeing. When I take the dog for a walk, I can be head-down, mind elsewhere, or I can look up and focus on what's around me. When I stop to notice my surroundings, I can't help but appreciate what's around me – the sky, the trees, the birds – and be grateful. I find it a real struggle to give thanks because I see the half-empty glass in front of me, rather than the half-full one. But even for the optimists among us, society constantly reminds us what we don't have but should be trying to get (a better job, a bigger house, the latest gadget) rather than being grateful for what we already have. After all, no salesperson ever made money from telling someone they've already got everything they could ever possibly need.

The Bible tells us to 'give thanks in all circumstances' (1 Thess. 5:18), and it should be no surprise to us that if God wants us to do it, it's very good for us. But this advice comes from elsewhere, too. Carl Vernon, author of *Anxiety Rebalance*[4] says 'gratitude is nature's solution to anxiety'. One of the reasons for this is that your brain can't be both grateful and anxious at the same time. Gratefulness can reduce stress and symptoms of depression, and the more often we practice it, the more sensitive it makes us to gratitude further down the line.[5]

Being thankful doesn't mean pretending that life is fantastic when we're in the midst of pain, but acknowledging that, while life is always going to be difficult, God is always good, and there are always many things to be thankful for. It's easy to take things for granted – a home, our health, our loved ones – until they are taken away, and then we realise just how much we appreciate them. It's not just the big things in our lives, but learning to be grateful for the small everyday blessings that God gives us. Diane and I have started a new habit of listing three things we're grateful for before we go to sleep each night. No matter how bad a day has been, how many challenges there are, there are always things to be thankful for if we pay attention.

TAKING OUR THOUGHTS CAPTIVE

Mindfulness might be fashionable at the moment, but the idea of being present in the moment isn't a new idea. One of the strengths of mindfulness is that it helps us study the thoughts going through our minds that are often left unchecked. Sometimes ideas and attitudes are so ingrained in our thinking that we don't even consider challenging them. We can forget that our thoughts might be opinions (about ourselves, others, circumstances, etc) rather than actual, evidence-based facts. We can challenge our thoughts, and not just passively accept them:

'We demolish arguments and every pretension that sets itself up against the knowledge of God, and we take captive every thought to make it obedient to Christ.' **(2 Cor. 10:5)**

It is estimated that, on average, we speak or hear around 500 words per minute – which might seem like a lot, but the self-talk going on in the subconscious mind averages a staggering

1,500 words a minute. That's a huge number of thoughts often going unchecked, and many of us will find they are often negative. A good strategy is to actually pay attention to our negative thoughts and ask ourselves: 'What would my best friend say to me in this situation?'

Many people have found cognitive behavioural therapy (CBT) helpful, which helps you identify negative thoughts. You take a thought and examine it, looking at what actual evidence there is to support it, and then list the evidence against it. Having done so, you can 'write' a new, more balanced thought to replace the original. This helps to give you another perspective, rather than your default unchecked one.

We need to realise that our thoughts are not always our friends, and they are often not even reality. When negativity hits, question the thought. If you don't feel strong enough to do this on your own then ask a close friend to help. When suffering with severe depression, author Byron Katie made this discovery:

'A thought is harmless unless we believe it. It's not our thoughts that cause suffering. Attaching to a thought means believing that it is true, without inquiring. A belief is a thought that we've been attaching to, often for years.'[6]

Another strategy is to spend time imagining an anxiety-free life. People who struggle with anxiety have amazing imaginations, which makes it easy to think through worst case scenarios. Chloe Botheridge, author of *The Anxiety Solution*, suggests this:

> *'You can use your imagination as a force for good. When you mentally rehearse a situation that typically makes you anxious, imagining things turning out fine and handling the hiccups along the way all the while remaining relaxed, you create new neural pathways in your brain that correspond with feeling relaxed when real life situations come about.'*[7]

Mindfulness researcher and Baptist minister Shaun Lambert says a shift in perspective can be helpful: 'Instead of looking at life *from* our thoughts, we look *at* our thoughts' (emphasis added). Stopping to ask ourselves why we're thinking a certain way, especially when it's a negative thought directed at ourselves, is the starting point for exploring an alternative opinion. Lambert continues: 'This verse [2 Cor. 10:5] enables us to witness our thoughts and enables us to decentre from them, to disarm them, notice them and then to let them go.'[8] To take our thoughts captive, we have to get curious about them, explore them and rid them of their malicious sting by showing ourselves they are untrue. Some experts say it's helpful to picture these thoughts like a leaf that we can let float away on a stream, or a train that we watch depart from a station, to aid the process of letting go. Another thought may arrive a second later, but it's important to just go through the same process again, and not start to feel swamped or like you'll never get a handle on your thoughts.

Although a floating leaf sounds lovely, all of this is very hard work – and I know this first-hand. My mind is a mincfield. My imagination can easily jump into soap opera mode once

I let my thoughts get the best of me, my speciality being imagining all sorts of worst case scenarios for my health and for my kids. I am very much a work in progress in this area, but I am starting to question the negative voices, which means they don't suck me in straightaway anymore. I recognise that my inner monologue contains a lot self-criticism, and it's often very accusing in nature. I know that I take too much responsibility for things I can't resolve, and I realise that my fear of disappointment has stopped me from allowing hope to blossom where it should. These thoughts have been as habitual to me as brushing my teeth but slowly, over time and with considerable effort, I am changing the thought patterns in my head.

Kristin Neff says that mindfulness is key to understanding self-compassion. She says it is 'taking a balanced approach to negative emotions so that feelings are neither suppressed nor exaggerated. We cannot ignore our pain and feel compassion for it at the same time. Mindfulness requires that we not "over identify" with thoughts and feelings, so that we are caught up and swept away by negativity.'[9]

Our thoughts are not always our friends. Let's be prepared to question them.

OUR GREATEST WEAPON

Our greatest weapon for fighting the lies in our heads is the Word of God. This is seen so vividly in the way that Jesus handled the temptations of the devil (Matt. 4; Luke 4). Theologian N.T. Wright says he doesn't envisage Jesus actually engaging in a conversation with a visible figure, but rather that the devil appeared in His head.[10] The battle was in His mind. Jesus overcame by listening to a different voice. Before He entered the wilderness, He had heard God telling Him He was His beloved Son. He knew His identity, but the devil's aim was to attack exactly what God had just told Him. The snide whisper of the enemy began with 'If you are…', so Jesus had to choose who to listen to, just like we do. Each time the voice came, Jesus hit back with Scripture, knowing that was the truth He could depend on.

The key to changing our mindsets is to meditate on the Word of God. Eastern meditation is about emptying your mind, whereas Christian meditation is about filling our minds up with God. Jesus was totally focused on the cross, and Satan's aim was to distract Him. Satan was offering a faster way for Jesus to accomplish His mission, tempting Him to forget the cross, forget the pain and suffering ahead, and to have it all in an instant. In many ways, Satan was offering Jesus the chance to be the Messiah the people wanted – the one who wielded power and took control – but Jesus knew there was a better way. And notice that He didn't respond by arguing. Arguing with temptation often means we play with the idea until it becomes too attractive to turn down. Jesus' focus was that God's kingdom would come, and His will be done. That's what enabled Him to stand up against the devil's lies.

The more we know who God is and who He says we are, the easier we will find it to hold on to the truth and let the lies go. We don't *need* dramatic encounters with God at festivals, or words from recognised prophets to grab a hold of this truth.

Let's slow down and become aware of the thoughts in our minds. Let's come back to God's Word and to seek Him on a daily basis. Let's hold our negative thoughts before Him, and ask Him to speak truth to us. This way, bit by bit, we allow Him to form our identity.

CHAPTER 10

BEING AUTHENTIC

Abigail was only ten weeks old when she started showing signs of an ear infection, but the doctor examining her told Diane that she wasn't sure Abigail could *see*. Diane was totally confused – she'd seemed fine to us. Then the doctor held a small pen above Abigail's face and moved it around, but Abigail's eyes didn't follow it. The doctor pointed out the constant flickering in Abigail's eyes, from left to right. We had noticed this, but thought it was just her way of taking everything in; apparently it was a sign she could have something called nystagmus. Follow-up appointments were made, and the diagnosis was confirmed.

The information we received said nystagmus is a condition affecting vision, where the eyes make repetitive, uncontrolled movements. These movements often result in reduced vision and depth perception, and can affect balance and co-ordination. The literature we were given said, 'If you've just had your child diagnosed with nystagmus, it's not the end of the world'. We tried to take comfort from that, but it still felt like the world we knew was crashing around us – not least of all because the condition can sometimes be caused by a more serious underlying problem such as a brain tumour or epilepsy.

Then Abigail had to have a series of tests. The first time she was quite sleepy and calm so didn't seem to mind. But the second time she was alert and upset, trying to pull the electrodes from her head, crying out loudly and looking completely bewildered. Her eyes and her screams questioned why we were doing this to her, and of course she was too young for us to explain.

Eventually the doctors concluded that there was no underlying cause to Abigail's nystagmus: it was just one of those things. We were told that her brain and eyes were healthy; it was the messages between the two that weren't working properly. Although this was good news, we still felt heartbroken at the thought of Abi having severely reduced vision. Glasses make no difference to nystagmus.

That wasn't the end of Abigail's challenges. As a toddler, she was extremely demanding and had terrible tantrums. Rather than growing out of them, the older she got, the worse they became. We felt like we tried every parenting and behavioural technique there was, but none of them seemed to work. By the time she reached school she was mostly well behaved and the school had no concerns, despite the fact she was at the bottom of the class academically. We were told there was a wide range of acceptable academic results at her age, and they believed she would catch up with her classmates by the time she was eight.

But we also had other concerns about Abi's behaviour. She would get very anxious and stressed, and though she could cope with behaving well at school, by the time she got home she would have a meltdown over the smallest thing.

It was exhausting not knowing what each day would bring and how best to help her, so eventually Diane took Abi to the doctors. The next five years were filled with appointments, tests and screenings, while Diane assembled a thick folder of paperwork that tried to help us understand what our little girl was dealing with. All of the specialists agreed that although Abigail definitely displayed symptoms, she didn't tick all the boxes for anything specific, and so they were unable to give her a definite label. She had her own 'box', and was therefore given the diagnosis of 'complex special needs'. This has been an extremely frustrating process. Some days she seems like any other child and we've wondered if we've got it wrong; on other days, things are so hard that we think it's not just Abigail who needs special support – so do we!

One night Diane and Abi were reading the book *Giraffes Can't Dance*.[1] It's about a giraffe in the jungle called Gerald, who is laughed at when he goes to the annual dance because everyone knows 'giraffes can't dance'. Feeling sad, Gerald starts walking home when he's stopped by a cricket, who challenges Gerald to try dancing again but with different music. It works, and Gerald ends up being the best dancer in the jungle. When Diane finished the story, Abigail excitedly said that the story was all about her. When asked what she meant, Abi explained that people think she can't do most things when she can – she just needs to find a different way to do it. It was a very special moment for all of us.

Abigail's emotions are incredibly intense. She feels things very deeply – so when she's sad, it's a deep and heavy sadness, and rather than worrying a little bit, she gets extreme anxiety.

The anxiety has such a grip on her that a simple choice (over what shoes to wear, for example) becomes something much more stressful. She worries that if she chooses one shoe over another, she will hurt the feelings of the un-chosen shoes, which can make getting ready a drawn out and painful process. But Abi's intense emotions also mean she has an amazing sense of what other people need, and she shows empathy in a way I have never seen in a child before. If someone comes to our house feeling lonely, hurting, or just needing some TLC, Abigail will pick up on it straightaway, long before the rest of us have noticed. She has a way of making people feel special and valued. She also seems to hear God in an amazing way. If I am facing a dilemma and I need to hear God's wisdom, I'll ask her to pray. She often says, 'Hang on, Dad…', walks out of the room to pray, and comes back ready to give me just one word that speaks into my situation.

It's painful to see our little girl struggle at times, but we have learnt to celebrate the flipside of Abi's special needs. As Diane often says, 'You can't always plan life but you can choose how you respond to it.' There isn't always a happy ending, and we're often left with questions and doubts about where God is and what He's up to in our lives. But it's engaging with God in the mysteries of life that helps us through. Most people who I have spoken with over the years – the bereaved, the lonely, those living with cancer, depression and anxiety, single, married, divorced – have said to me: 'I choose to trust God even though I don't understand what's going on.'

MOVING BACK, MOVING FORWARDS

While we were fighting to get a diagnosis for Abi, Diane struggled with all the pressure she was under. Her closest friends had moved away from London over a period of a couple of years, and she was really feeling the lack of support. One night, out of the blue, I said, 'I think God might be saying we need to move back to be near our parents.' I couldn't believe what was coming out of my mouth. I had lived in London for 23 years and loved it. I had no desire to live anywhere else.

I love how multicultural London is; I love the vibrancy of Peckham and the resilient community spirit it has. London was the place where I had invested so much of myself; I had worked in most of the local schools over the years as well as starting projects on multiple local housing estates. Chelmsford, where our parents live, is only about an hour and half away from Peckham but it's like another world. I had good memories of growing up there, but all my friends had long since moved away or we'd lost touch.

My prayers in the following weeks largely consisted of asking God to take this thought away, and make it clear that it was just my imagination and not His voice. I just couldn't see how I could run XLP from Chelmsford. Bizarrely, the train journey would actually be quicker than from Peckham, but I was concerned that there would be no authenticity in my working with young people in London if I wasn't living there myself. One of my core values is integrity, and I need to be able to speak with understanding and authority on the issues that inner-city communities face, rather than popping in from my comfortable suburban home.

I was so conflicted, but I could see that Diane was struggling to cope, and I knew life would be so much easier with both sets of parents on the doorstep. I saw Abigail struggling to get the one-on-one attention she needed from us and at her school. I realised that being authentic meant putting my family first, ahead of my ministry. Diane had made so many sacrifices for me over the years, as had my family in Chelmsford. It was time for a drastic change.

As we started looking at houses near our parents, I began to see how much of my identity was wrapped up in living in Peckham. I liked telling people that's where I lived, perhaps because Peckham has a bit of a reputation and it makes me look tougher than I am. But what good is having a reputation if your family is falling apart under pressure? Why hold on to the things God called you to years before, when He's started saying something new?

I talked everything through with my mentor, and he told me a story about the singer Lionel Richie. When Lionel was too young to read he used a water fountain that had a 'white only' sign above it. A group of four white guys started harassing Lionel's dad who was with him and Lionel watched, thinking his military dad would 'kick their asses'. But his dad said nothing. It bothered Lionel for a long time, wondering why his dad had acted so cowardly. So years later he talked to his dad about that day, and asked why he didn't stand up to them. His dad said, 'I had a choice that day of either being a man or your father. I knew if I fought them they would kill me and I chose to be your dad.'[2] My mentor said to me, 'Patrick, you worry about integrity and being authentic all the time and that's admirable, but go and be an authentic dad, husband and son.'

It's so easy to put our work for God first and not realise when we are neglecting our families in the process. We may be physically there with them, but we are often emotionally and mentally unavailable due to the other demands we face. My family doesn't need me to have a messiah complex. They don't need me to be a hero; they just need me to be a good dad. Integrity is practising what we preach behind the scenes and behind closed doors. That is living authentically in the season God has us in.

LETTING GO

In my 21 years at XLP, people often jokingly said, 'You're never allowed to leave!' I've made my fair share of mistakes and unpopular decisions, but I think those words highlighted people's desire for a sense of stability for the charity and, to be honest, I couldn't imagine being anywhere else. But I heard God clearly telling me it was time to let go of XLP, and He began speaking to me about new things. I immediately had a hundred questions: how could I walk away from XLP when it is like a child to me? How would I feel about giving over final decisions to someone else? How would I cope with losing my office, my PA, and my support structures? Would I lose my friends on the staff, who I've grown close to? Yet I knew that just as we relate to our parents differently when we become adults, it was time for me to step back.

Some of the issues raised by the prospect of moving on flagged up some deeper questions in me, such as where is my security? How would I feel if I didn't have a big organisation backing me? Would my leaving have a negative effect on the work of the charity? I was overwhelmed with questions and guilt that I couldn't shake, and my anxiety was starting to spiral out of control. I thought that I held XLP lightly, but now I could see how strongly I was attached to it. Was God really calling me to let it go?

And what about stepping into a new adventure? Though finances at XLP have never been easy, at least my salary had been fairly secure. Diane and I have four kids and a mortgage. Surely God wasn't asking me to start something new and live with that level of uncertainty again? Surely pioneering something *once* in your life is enough?

As I started to tell some trusted friends what I thought God might be saying, one sent me this quote from Brennan Manning:

> 'The way of trust is a movement into obscurity, into the undefined, into ambiguity, not into some predetermined, clearly delineated plan for the future. The next step discloses itself only out of a discernment of God acting in the desert of the present moment. The reality of naked trust is the life of the pilgrim who leaves what is nailed down, obvious, and secure, and walks into the unknown without any rational explanation to justify the decision or guarantee the future. Why? Because God has signalled the movement and offered it his presence and his promise.'[3]

It felt like God was calling me to trust Him at a deeper level than I had experienced before: that He was calling me to go not only to the broken places around the world that I had been so fond of, but to the broken places within me; the parts I would rather leave buried than have to deal with. I've often spoken about courage and vulnerability being the same thing (inspired by the amazing Brené Brown), yet this seemed to be on a totally different level. Deep down, I knew I was on a journey of letting go. Not letting go for no reason, but letting go in order to be more authentic and to receive more of God's love; to remember again that He is often more interested in what I am becoming than what I am doing. Like many people, I crave certainty. I want everything nailed down. I don't like waiting and I certainly don't like being still, yet God wasn't giving me detailed instructions of the next steps. I wanted a map, but He was offering me Himself.

When everything is stripped back, we start to realise what is really important: our ability to give and receive love. We can learn to let go of the things we've picked up over the years: the unhelpful thinking patterns, and the need for affirmation from others to prove that we are somehow a good person. We can grow in humility. We can deepen our friendships, learning to rely on others in a healthy way. We can identify where our limitations are – and that it's actually OK to have limitations. We realise we're not the only ones struggling and there are many others who want to join the journey, longing for a faith that has a depth to it, that can handle the tough questions arising out of baffling circumstances.

THE WILDERNESS

As I've said goodbye to XLP, I've felt like I'm heading out into the wilderness with no props, no title and no big team to hide behind – yet I am strangely excited. I realise that in the wilderness, I have to be real. I have to be authentic. It can be a place where we experience real closeness to God as we depend on Him, and increased intimacy with others when we journey together. Where there is space, there is room for creativity. The wilderness in the Bible was a place where God revealed Himself time and time again. It was at the burning bush in the wilderness that Moses got his new job description. (In fact, Moses spent most of his time in the wilderness.) As Brené Brown describes so eloquently, it's a place where God longs to heal us, mould and shape us into the people He created us to be:

> 'You will be shocked how many people live out there –
> thriving, dancing, creating, celebrating, and belonging.
> It is not void of human flourishing. The wilderness is where
> all the creatives and prophets and system buckers and risk
> takers have always lived and it is stunningly vibrant. The
> walk out there is hard, but authenticity out there is life.'[4]

One of my favourite Bible verses is Song of Songs 8:5: 'Who is this coming up from the wilderness leaning on her beloved?' If you are leaning on someone, you need to trust him or her and you need to be able to admit that you need their help. In this season of heading out into the unknown, I'm longing to lean on Jesus, to trust that He is willing and able to hold me up, guide and direct me. I'm holding on to Him with all I have, letting go of the past and embracing whatever He has for me in the future.

CHAPTER 11

BEING HOPEFUL

As I look back over the last couple of decades, I can see how God has been using some of the challenges I've been through to prepare me for what's ahead. When I finally made the decision to move on from XLP, it felt like I was confronted with all my brokenness at the same time, yet there was something beautiful emerging from within me – something far more personal that went deeper than anything I'd experienced before. I've always wanted to be someone who leads with honesty, able to admit my weaknesses whether with my friends, in front of my team or standing on a stage preaching. But I needed to go even further if I was to be truly authentic.

At times I've wondered if I should have toned down some of the things I've said here or in *When Faith Gets Shaken*. I've worried about how people will judge me if they see the behind-the-scenes reality of my life and not just the glossy highlights reel. I've felt shame creep in because of my failings and weaknesses and I've wanted to hide myself away. I've sometimes felt isolated, wondering if I'm the only one who struggles in these areas, assuming that others will be convinced that I'm having a crisis of faith. I've heard the lying whisper that tells me I should be stronger and better able to cope. But I want to be someone who leads because of my vulnerability, not despite it. I don't want to be afraid of being a weak leader; I want my weakness to reveal a strong God.

Throughout all of our doubts and questions, Diane and I spent a lot of time talking about the need to be open about our struggles to help other people feel less alone in theirs. We started to dream about how we could support others who are dealing with life's challenges. We wanted to reach people of faith and those with none, because we all struggle with areas of pain in our lives.

A plan started to take shape to write course material that could be delivered in churches, prisons, coffee shops, schools and more, looking at themes such as acceptance, community, honesty, patience, anxiety and depression. I got excited at the idea of doing an *Honesty Over Silence* speaking tour with Diane to try to open up conversations around the topics in this book. Amazingly, my friends at CWR were keen to partner with us and provide access to counselling services in support of this.[1] We started to talk about the fact that brokenness isn't just an individual experience, but something entire communities can face. We wanted to find a way to support and help develop projects with partners who are creating hope for others in struggling communities, whether here in the UK or overseas.

Jamaica, for example, is an amazing country with amazing people, yet communities are being torn apart by gang violence. Many of the young people I met while working there had been traumatised by what they had experienced. Around 90% of the children in a school I regularly visited didn't have a dad, and some were also without mothers, instead being brought up by aunties or other family members. Abuse can be very high as child protection laws are not enforced in Jamaica, and as a result, the children can develop lots of mental health issues. I long to see these young people get the support they so desperately need, through initiatives such as having counsellors on staff in the schools. In many countries where war and violence are prevalent, young people's mental health inevitably suffers. We often send food, clothing and medical supplies, but what do we do to help young people deal with the trauma they have witnessed and been subjected to? What will life be like for those young people in five years' time if we don't do anything to support their mental wellbeing now?

Diane and I were both equally passionate about all of these issues, and wanted to work on finding answers together. We could see that we needed to start a whole new charity to be an umbrella for all the things we wanted to do, but knew that would be a huge challenge. I had yet more questions: would I cope with going from having the support of a big team at XLP, to it being just Diane and me? How would we raise the money we needed, especially when I don't really like fundraising? Would we be able to support our family and pay our mortgage? Was I strong enough to do this, or did I need to be further along in my journey of healing?

Despite everything that could go wrong, we took the plunge and started a charity. Diane suggested we called it Kintsugi Hope, in reference to the Japanese art of mending cracked pots using a gold glue, to make a feature of the broken places instead of trying to hide them. We felt that this perfectly articulates the truth that we shouldn't try and hide our broken places, and that they can even make our lives more beautiful. We made a short video of a number of us trying the art of kintsugi to help explain the charity's vision, and I realised first-hand that it's not something to be rushed. It takes care, patience and a gentle touch. Seeing the finished pieces was a stunning reminder that God uses our scars; He is the master of turning something painful into something purposeful.

When we began to talk to other people about Kintsugi Hope, it sparked deep conversations in pubs, at the schools gates and in coffee shops. Friends began to open up about things that had happened to them, and some of the pain they were feeling or that their loved ones were experiencing. They often said things like, 'I have never told anyone this before', and that's what it's all about: initiating these kinds of conversations, which so desperately need to happen. Our prayer is that Kintsugi Hope will beautifully and creatively reflect the kingdom of God, where it's not the strong who are given a place of honour but the weak, the orphans, the widows, the broken and the marginalised who are elevated to front and centre.

Hope is the second part of the charity's name because it's so central to the healing journey. It's not about having hope that everything will turn out well – we won't have happy endings to every story in our lives, and we'll all carry elements of brokenness until we enter the kingdom of God. Hope is a choice, and it's about something far deeper than an optimistic outlook on life. Charles Snyder, who dedicated his whole career to studying hope, said, 'Hope isn't emotion, it is a way of thinking or a cognitive process.'[2]

HOPE IN THE DARKEST PLACES

One story that has inspired me so much in the area of hope is that of Corrie ten Boom. For those not familiar with the story, the ten Boom family were Christians and watchmakers who lived in Haarlem, Amsterdam. When the Nazis invaded Europe, the family took the risky decision to open their home to persecuted Jews. They put a false wall in Corrie's bedroom, where people could hide until it was safe to go into hiding elsewhere. They saved hundreds of lives, and the ten Boom house became a centre of underground activities. But in 1944, the family were arrested and Corrie and her sister, Betsie, were eventually taken to the Ravensbrück concentration camp – notorious for being one of the worst.

Conditions were horrendous: filthy and cold, the women were starved and humiliated, crammed into tiny sleeping bunks where lice would eat away at their skin. Roll call was at 4:30am and could last up to three hours as Corrie and Betsie stood in front of the guards, freezing and muttering under their breath the words of Romans 8:35: 'Who shall separate us from the love of Christ? Shall trouble or hardship or persecution or famine or nakedness or danger or sword?' One morning, a fellow prisoner was so malnourished and abused that she didn't have the strength to stand during roll call, and fell directly in front of Corrie. As the guards commanded her to get up, a skylark appeared. The skylark is one of the only birds to sing in the darkness, and Corrie described it like this:

'The sweet, pure notes of the bird rose on the still cold air.
Every head turned upward, away from the carnage before

> *us, listening to the song of the skylark soaring over the crematorium. The word of the psalmist ran through my mind: "For as the heaven is high above the earth, so great is [God's] mercy towards them that fear Him" (Psalms 103:11). I looked out at the men who were sitting in front of me. No longer were their faces filled with darkness and anger. They were listening – intently – for they were hearing from someone who had walked where they were now walking… There in that prison I saw things from God's point of view. The reality of God's love was just as sure as the cruelty of men.'[3]*

The story of the skylark really gets to me. Can we be people who sing not only in the great times in our lives but also in the places of darkness? What song is God calling us to sing, knowing that one day everything will be put right and pain will be gone forever? Kay Warren, who has known something of pain and depression in her own life, says that life isn't so much like mountains and valleys, but two railway tracks that run alongside each other. There is always one track with good stuff running through our lives, and equally there will always be a track with bad stuff too. When you follow the train tracks and look into the distance, when they reach the horizon, they become one. We will always have loss and sadness to some degree in this life, but one day God will wipe away every tear, heal every sickness and rid us of every pain as He restores this world (Rev. 21). Only the train track full of joy will remain, and we will be reconciled with God.[4]

THE DARK THREADS

Before we started Kintsugi Hope, Diane and I visited Haarlem to go to Corrie ten Boom's house, which has been turned into a museum. The atmosphere in the house was beautiful. We sat and listened to stories of the ten Boom family, and saw the false wall the Jewish families were hidden behind and the living area that was kept just as it had been during the war. After we'd seen the house, one of the volunteers held up a picture. I couldn't make out what it was – it just looked like a mess of threads overlapping. The guide told us that after giving a talk, Corrie used to hold up this picture and read this poem by Grant Colfax Tullar:

'My life is like a weaving
Between my Lord and me;
I cannot choose the colors
He worketh steadily.

Oft times he weaveth sorrow
And I, in foolish pride,
Forget He sees the upper,
And I the underside.

Not 'til the loom is silent
And the shuttles cease to fly,
Will God unroll the canvas
And reveal the reason why.

The dark threads are needful
In the Weaver's skilful hand,
As the threads of gold and silver
In the pattern He has planned.

He knows, He loves, He cares,
Nothing this truth can dim.
He gives His very best to those
Who choose to walk with Him.'[5]

We'd been looking at the back of a tapestry. When the guide turned it round, the picture was clearly of a precious crown. That inspires me. God is at work in our lives. Though we see the mess behind the scenes; though we don't always understand the light and shade we experience; though life looks confusing and feels painful; we can still trust. We offer up our lives to the creator: He takes each and every strand, the good and the bad, and He weaves in each of us a masterpiece.

AFTERWORD

I am so grateful to you for going on this journey with me and reading this book. My prayer for you is that you will know that you don't have to wear a pretend smile. I hope you know that being vulnerable and being able to lament are acts of great courage, rather than signs of weakness. I hope you find a way to accept your brokenness in order that you might move forward in your healing.

If you suffer from anxiety, depression or any other mental health issue, I pray you would know that you have nothing to be ashamed of. I pray you would allow God to come into the areas of your past that have caused you pain, so that He can bring His love and healing.

I pray you will be able to practise self-compassion, treating yourself with the kindness and care you extend to others, mindful of the thoughts you allow to take root. I hope you will find true community where you can lean on others, have them lean on you, and know you are loved for who you are.

Whatever circumstances you're dealing with that are causing you pain, I pray you will know God close. Know that He is always with you, He is always at work, and there is always hope. May you know that you are not alone, no matter what you are facing. May we be a body of believers who cheer each other on.

May your life be one marked by the fact that your greatest concern is knowing the love of God in increasing measure, and of expressing that love to those around you.

On the day we got the Kintsugi Hope charity number through from the Charity Commission, I wrote these words in my journal:

'Here's to the future, to speaking to the broken, the lonely, the outcasts, the scared, to those who don't know how valuable they are, the traumatised refugee, the abused school kids in Trenchtown, the anxious, the depressed, those who feel stigmatised, and those who feel they can't lift their head up high. We're not coming with patronising messages or black and white answers but with love; reaching out our hand to grab yours, to walk alongside you for a while to whisper into your ears how precious you are and that you are made in the image of a God who loves you. You are enough. You belong and you will discover treasure in those scars.

I am done with trying to find quick fixes, with insecurities driving my actions, with not being vulnerable. We don't want to play it safe. We're going to take a walk into the wilderness and know it's OK to be out there, being true to ourselves and following God's call, knowing it's the best place to be. Let's embrace integrity, risk-taking and authenticity. Bring on the wrestling – it's time for a new journey to begin.'

ENDNOTES

CHAPTER 1

[1] Brené Brown, *Daring Greatly* (New York: Penguin, 2012)

[2] Mark Yaconelli, *Disappointment, Doubt and Other Spiritual Gifts* (London: SPCK, 2016) p102

[3] Barbara Brown Taylor, *Learning to Walk in the Dark* (New York: HarperCollins, 2014) p5

CHAPTER 2

[1] This was taken from a blog post by poet Kirsten Corley, called 'What Anxiety Actually is, Because It's More Than Just Worrying', hosted by thoughtcatalogue.com (I don't wish to endorse the other content on Coley's blog, but I found her summary of anxiety very illuminating.)

[2] Archbishop Desmond Tutu, *Book of Joy* (London: Penguin, 2016) p224

[3] Taken from an article called 'Henri Nouwen: Writings' by Henri J.M. Nouwen and Robert A. Jonas, found at *Spirituality & Practice: Resources for spiritual journeys* (www.spiritualityandpractice.com/book-reviews), accessed March 2018.

[4] Henri Nouwen, *The Inner Voice of Love* (New York: Doubleday, 1998)

CHAPTER 3

[1] Pete Greig, *Dirty Glory: Go Where Your Best Prayers Take You* (London: Hodder & Stoughton, 2016) p142

[2] Nicky Gumbel, @nickygumbel Twitter post: 12:48pm, 7 January 2018

[3] Gene Weingarten, 'Pearls Before Breakfast', *Washington Post*, published 8 April 2007 (www.washingtonpost.com), accessed March 2018.

CHAPTER 4

[1] World Health Organisation, 'I had a black dog, his name was depression', video written and illustrated by Matthew Johnstone (published 2 October 2012), accessed via YouTube, March 2018.

[2] Information and statistics supplied by Mind (www.mind.org.uk), accessed March 2018.

[3] This is taken from a helpful blog called *Blurt: Increasing Awareness and Understanding of Depression*, which can be found at www.blurtitout.org (search for 'Ten Lies') accessed March 2018.

[4] Christy Wimber, *Transformed* (Venice, CA, USA: Monarch Books, 2017), p96

[5] Taken from an interview with Rick and Kay Warren at the 2014 HTB Leadership Conference (5 May 2014) at the Royal Albert Hall, accessed via YouTube, March 2018.

[6] *Ibid.*

[7] Dr Tim Cantopher, *Depressive Illness: The Curse of the Strong* (London: Sheldon Press, 2003) p6

[8] Roger Steer, *Hudson Taylor: A Man in Christ* (Milton Keynes: Authentic Media and OMF, 1990) p233

[9] *Ibid.*, p236

[10] Chris Ledger and Wendy Bray, *Insight into Depression* (Farnham: CWR, 2009) p36

CHAPTER 5

[1] *Only Fools and Horses*, 'Time on Our Hands', Season 7, Episode 13 (BBC, 1981–2003)

[2] Information found at www.tommys.org, accessed March 2018.

[3] Brené Brown, *Braving the Wilderness* (New York: Penguin RandomHouse, 2017) p67

[4] Wm Paul Young, *The Shack* (Newbury Park, CA, USA: Windblown Media, 2007) p97

[5] Tim Keller, *Walking with God through Pain and Suffering* (New York: Hodder & Stoughton, 2013) p260

CHAPTER 6

[1] Dr Kristin Neff, 'Definition of Self-Compassion' (www.self-compassion.org). You can also watch a brilliant TEDx Talk by Neff, 'The Space Between Self-Esteem and Self-Compassion', found on the TEDx YouTube channel, originally published 6 February 2013, both accessed March 2018.

[2] Sheryl Sandberg and Adam Grant, *Option B: Facing Adversity, Building Resilience, and Finding Joy* (New York: Virgin/WH Allen, 2017), Kindle edition

[3] Anne Wilson Schaef, *Meditations for Women Who Do Too Much* (New York: HarperOne, 1990)

[4] Will van der Hart, *Perfectionism* (London: IVP, 2006) p52

[5] Charles Stanley, *The Spirit-Filled life: Discovering the Joy of Surrendering to the Holy Spirit* (New York: Thomas Nelson, 2014) p6

RACHEL'S STORY

[1] Rachel Wright, *The Skies I'm Under* (Great Britain: Born at the Right Time Publishing, 2017). You can also read more from Rachel on her blog: www.bornattherighttime.com

[2] Viktor Frankl, *Man's Search For Meaning* (New York: Pocket Books, 1984)

[3] Sheryl Sandberg and Adam Grant, *ibid.*

[4] Barbara Brown Taylor, *Leaving Church: A Memoir of Faith* (New York: HarperCollins, 2006)

CHAPTER 7

[1] Philip Yancey, *Vanishing Grace* (London: Hodder & Stoughton, 2014) pp93–94

[2] John Powell, *Why Am I Afraid to Tell You Who I Am?* (Grand Rapids, MI, USA: Zondervan, 1999) p12

[3] Trevor J. Partridge, *Love With Skin On* (Farnham: CWR, 2016) p35

[4] Johann Hari, 'Is everything you think you know about depression wrong?', *The Guardian*, 7 January 2018, www.theguardian.com, accessed March 2018.

[5] Anushka Asthana, 'Stories of loneliness: two MPs tell of "social epidemic" in the UK', *The Guardian*, 3 January 2018, www.theguardian.com, accessed March 2018. This research was done by a Conservative MP and a Labour MP working together to honour the work of murdered MP Jo Cox, to demonstrate her words that 'we have more in common than that which divides us'.

[6] Brené Brown gave this brilliant talk on empathy, which you can find on the RSA YouTube channel, accessed March 2018.

[7] Samuel Wells and Marcia A. Owen, *Living Without Enemies: Being Present in the Midst of Violence* (Downers Grove, IL, USA: IVP Books, 2010) p30

CHAPTER 8

[1] Henri Nouwen, *The Return of the Prodigal Son* (New York: Doubleday, 1992) p43

[2] The blog of the Reverend Doctor Daniel DeForest London can be found at www.deforestlondon.wordpress.com, accessed March 2018. This quote was taken from the post called 'A Palestinian perspective on the prodigal son'.

[3] Elie Wiesel, *Night* (New York: Penguin Books, 1972) xx

[4] Timothy Keller, *The Prodigal God: Recovering the Heart of the Christian Faith* (London: Hodder & Stoughton, 2009)

[5] The story of Dominique Voillaume was cited in Brennan Manning, *The Signature of Jesus: Living a Life of Holy Passion and Unreasonable Faith* (Colorado Springs, CO, USA: Multnomah Press, 2004) p98

CHAPTER 9

[1] Michael Yaconelli, *Messy Spirituality* (London: Hodder & Stoughton, 2001) p110

[2] John Ortberg, *Soul Keeping* (Grand Rapids, MI, USA: Zondervan, 2014) p20

[3] Trevor J. Partridge, *ibid.*, p87

[4] Carl Vernon, *Anxiety Rebalance: All the Answers You Need to Overcome Anxiety and Depression* (London: Headline, 2016)

[5] 'Practicing Gratitude can be Good for Mental Health and Well-Being' (published 4 August 2017), *American Psychiatric Association*, www.psychiatry.org, accessed March 2018.

[6] Byron Katie, *Loving What Is: Four Questions That Can Change Your Life* (New York: Harmony Books, 2003)

[7] Chloe Botheridge, *The Anxiety Solution – a Quieter Mind, a Calmer You* (London: Michael Joseph, 2017) p189

[8] Shaun Lambert, *A Book of Sparks: A Study in Christian Mindfullness* (Watford: Instant Apostle, 2014)

[9] Kristin Neff, *Self Compassion: Stop Beating Yourself Up and Leave Insecurity Behind* (New York: William Morrow, 2011), cited in Brené Brown, *Daring Greatly* (New York: Penguin, 2012)

[10] N.T. Wright, *Luke For Everyone* (London: SPCK, 2001) p43

CHAPTER 10

[1] Giles Andreae and Guy Parker-Rees, *Giraffes Can't Dance* (London: Orchard Books, 1999)

[2] This story was originally shared with Piers Morgan on the TV programme *Life Stories*, and later recounted in an article by Mark Jefferies for *Daily Record*, originally published 3 September 2015 (www.dailyrecord.co.uk/entertainment), accessed March 2018.

[3] Brennan Manning, *Ruthless Trust: The Ragamuffin's Path to God* (New York: HarperOne, 2002) p12

[4] Brené Brown, *Braving the Wilderness* (London: Vermilion, 2017) p152

CHAPTER 11

[1] CWR offers a 'Find a Counsellor' service – an online directory of qualified Christian counsellors who have trained through Waverley Abbey College. To access this tool, visit www.cwr.org.uk/findacounsellor to search your local area. The Waverley Abbey Insight Series provides resources and courses addressing a wide range of challenges, from depression and anxiety to bereavement, eating disorders, bullying, self-esteem and many more. For further details of the resources available, see www.cwr.org.uk/insight

[2] C.R. Snyder, *Psychology of Hope: You Can Get There From Here* (New York: Simon and Schuster, 2003)

[3] Corrie ten Boom with Jamie Buckingham, *Tramp for the Lord* (London: Hodder & Stoughton, 1972) p84

[4] Taken from Kay Warren's devotional series on YouTube, 'Choose Joy, Because Happiness Isn't Enough', published 16 May 2014, accessed March 2018.

[5] Found at www.corrietenboomfonds.com, accessed March 2018.

Kintsugi Hope was founded by Diane and Patrick Regan OBE, and exists to create safe and supportive spaces for those experiencing mental and emotional health challenges. We run community groups and events around the UK and can provide speakers for your church or gathering. We also work internationally to support people whose mental and emotional health has been affected by conflict, trauma and poverty, particularly within the refugee community.

Find out more about how you can get involved and support Kintsugi Hope at **www.kintsugihope.com** and keep in touch with the latest news on **www.facebook.com/kintsugihope** and Twitter **@KintsugiHope**

CWR Insight Series

Handling issues that are feared, ignored or misunderstood

Addiction   Bereavement   Disappointment
Stress Anger Child and Adult Bullying
Assertiveness **Forgiveness** Self-Acceptance
Perfectionism Depression **Anxiety**
Sexual Abuse Burnout Managing Conflict
Dementia **Eating Disorders**
Self-Esteem Self-Harm

Insight Days – These invaluable teaching days are designed both for those who would like to come for their own benefit and for those supporting others.

Insight Books – These books give biblical and professional insight into some of the key issues many people face today. Suitable for those facing the issues involved, as well as those supporting others, each book includes case studies and practical insights.

Find out more about Insight Days and books at
www.cwr.org.uk/insight

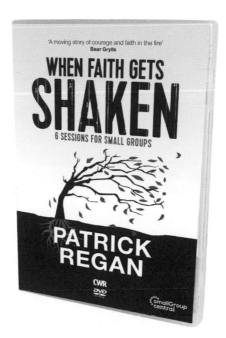

When Faith Gets Shaken DVD

Powerful interviews and honest reflections explore how we can keep going when we feel like everything is falling apart. Filmed on location in London, Patrick Regan shares his own journey through faith-shaking life experiences. Ideal for individuals and small groups.

Running time: 6 sessions of approx. 8–15 mins each, plus on-screen discussion starters.

EAN: 5027957-001633

Available from **www.cwr.org.uk/shop**
or from Christian bookshops.

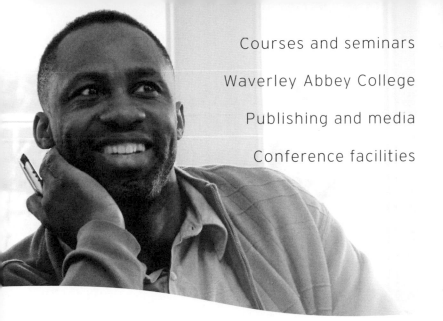

Courses and seminars

Waverley Abbey College

Publishing and media

Conference facilities

Transforming lives

CWR's vision is to enable people to experience personal transformation through applying God's Word to their lives and relationships.

Our Bible-based training and resources help people around the world to:
• Grow in their walk with God
• Understand and apply Scripture to their lives
• Resource themselves and their church
• Develop pastoral care and counselling skills
• Train for leadership
• Strengthen relationships, marriage and family life and much more.

Our insightful writers provide daily Bible reading notes and other resources for all ages, and our experienced course designers and presenters have gained an international reputation for excellence and effectiveness.

CWR's Training and Conference Centre in Surrey, England, provides excellent facilities in idyllic settings – ideal for both learning and spiritual refreshment.

CWR Applying God's Word to everyday life and relationships

CWR, Waverley Abbey House, Waverley Lane, Farnham, Surrey GU9 8EP, UK

Telephone: **+44 (0)1252 784700**
Email: **info@cwr.org.uk**
Website: **www.cwr.org.uk**

Registered Charity No. 294387
Company Registration No. 1990308